DEADLY DISEASES AND EPIDEMICS

ANTHRAX

DEADLY DISEASES AND EPIDEMICS

Anthrax

Cholera

Influenza

Polio

Syphilis

Tuberculosis

DEADLY DISEASES AND EPIDEMICS

ANTHRAX

Janet Decker

CONSULTING EDITOR
I. Edward Alcamo
Distinguished Teaching Professor of Microbiology,
SUNY Farmingdale

FORWORD BY
David Heymann
World Health Organization

CHELSEA HOUSE PUBLISHERS
A Haights Cross Communications Company
Philadelphia

Dedication

We dedicate the books in the DEADLY DISEASES AND EPIDEMICS series to Ed Alcamo, whose wit, charm, intelligence, and commitment to biology education were second to none.

CHELSEA HOUSE PUBLISHERS

VP, NEW PRODUCT DEVELOPMENT Sally Cheney
DIRECTOR OF PRODUCTION Kim Shinners
CREATIVE MANAGER Takeshi Takahashi
MANUFACTURING MANAGER Diann Grasse

Staff for Anthrax

ASSOCIATE EDITOR Beth Reger
ASSISTANT EDITOR Kate Sullivan
PRODUCTION EDITOR Jamie Winkler
PHOTO EDITOR Sarah Bloom
SERIES DESIGNER Terry Mallon
COVER DESIGNER Takeshi Takahashi
LAYOUT 21st Century Publishing and Communications, Inc.

A Haights Cross Communications Company

http://www.chelseahouse.com

First Printing

1 3 5 7 9 8 6 4 2

Library of Congress Cataloging-in-Publication Data

Decker, Janet M.
    Anthrax / Janet Decker.
       v. cm.—(Deadly diseases and epidemics)
Contents: A cloud of death—The fifth plague—Human anthrax—How anthrax causes disease—Dead letter (outbreak 2001)—Diagnosing and treating anthrax—Anthrax vaccine—Anthrax and bioterrorism.
    ISBN 0-7910-7302-5
    1. Anthrax—Juvenile literature. 2. Bioterrorism—Juvenile literature.
[1. Anthrax.] I. Title. II. Series.
RA644.A6 D43 2003
616.9'56—dc21

                                                              2002155987

Table of Contents

Foreword

In the 1960s, infectious diseases—which had terrorized generations—were tamed. Building on a century of discoveries, the leading killers of Americans both young and old were being prevented with new vaccines or cured with new medicines. The risk of death from pneumonia, tuberculosis, meningitis, influenza, whooping cough, and diphtheria declined dramatically. New vaccines lifted the fear that summer would bring polio, and a global campaign was approaching the global eradication of smallpox. New pesticides like DDT cleared mosquitoes from homes and fields, thus reducing the incidence of malaria which was present in the southern United States and a leading killer of children worldwide. New technologies produced safe drinking water and removed the risk of cholera and other water-borne diseases. Science seemed unstoppable. Disease seemed destined to almost disappear.

But the euphoria of the 1960s has evaporated.

Microbes fight back. Those causing diseases like TB and malaria evolved resistance to cheap and effective drugs. The mosquito evolved the ability to defuse pesticides. New diseases emerged, including AIDS, Legionnaires, and Lyme disease. And diseases which haven't been seen in decades re-emerge, as the hantavirus did in the Navajo Nation in 1993. Technology itself actually created new health risks. The global transportation network, for example, meant that diseases like West Nile virus could spread beyond isolated regions in distant countries and quickly become global threats. Even modern public health protections sometimes failed, as they did in Milwaukee, Wisconsin in 1993 which resulted in 400,000 cases of the digestive system illness cryptosporidiosis. And, more recently, the threat from smallpox, a disease completely eradicated, has returned along with other potential bioterrorism weapons such as anthrax.

The lesson is that the fight against infectious diseases will never end.

In this constant struggle against disease, we as individuals have a weapon that does not require vaccines or drugs, the warehouse of knowledge. We learn from the history of science that "modern" beliefs can be wrong. In this series of books, for example, you will learn that diseases like syphilis were once thought to be caused by eating potatoes. The invention of the microscope set science on the right path. There are more positive lessons from history. For example, smallpox was eliminated by vaccinating everyone who had come in contact with an infected person. This "ring" approach to controlling smallpox is still the preferred method for confronting a smallpox outbreak should the disease be intentionally reintroduced.

At the same time, we are constantly adding new drugs, new vaccines and new information to the warehouse. Recently, the entire human genome was decoded. So too was the genome of the parasite that causes malaria. Perhaps by looking at the microbe and the victim through the lens of genetics we will to be able to discover new ways of fighting malaria, still the leading killer of children in many countries.

Because of the knowledge gained about such diseases as AIDS, entire new classes of anti-retroviral drugs have been developed. But resistance to all these drugs has already been detected, so we know that AIDS drug development must continue.

Education, experimentation, and the discoveries which grow out of them are the best tools to protect health. Opening this book may put you on the path of discovery. I hope so, because new vaccines, new antibiotics, new technologies and, most importantly, new scientists are needed now more than ever if we are to remain on the winning side of this struggle with microbes.

David Heymann
Executive Director
Communicable Diseases Section
World Health Organization
Geneva, Switzerland

1

A Cloud of Death

November 1: It is a perfect night for football in the city of Northeast.[1]
Seventy-four thousand fans fill the downtown stadium to watch the game.
During the first quarter of the game, a truck drives along the elevated
highway a mile west of the stadium. Terrorists in the truck release an
odorless, invisible cloud of anthrax powder that drifts over the stadium on
the gentle breeze. Some of the powder blows beyond the stadium into
business and residential neighborhoods. By the end of the game, 16,000
people in the stadium and 4,000 farther east are infected. Unaware of
their danger, fans return to their homes in Northeast and surrounding
states. The anthrax delivery team is 100 miles away by the end of the game
and in another country by the next day (Figure 1.1).

November 3: Hundreds of people develop fevers and coughs. Some are
short of breath and have chest pains. Many assume they have the flu and
take over-the-counter medications. Others phone or visit their doctors,
who prescribe bed rest and fluids. A few are admitted to hospitals, where
they have chest x-rays, and their blood is tested for bacteria. Although
400 people are ill, no single doctor has seen a large number of cases. Since
cases of flu have been reported in the city during the past two weeks, the
diagnosis of flu seems reasonable.

November 4: As the number of ill people increases, health-care workers
contact the city health department for a flu update. Bacteria seen in some

---

1. This case study is adapted from "Anthrax: A Possible Case History" published by
   Thomas Inglesby in *Emerging Infectious Diseases* August, 1999.

Figure 1.1 Large cities, such as the one pictured here, and any place where many people congregate in a small area, such as a stadium or arena, are prime locations for the spread of an airborne disease. In the hypothetical scenario described in the text, a group of terrorists released anthrax spores into the air near the stadium. Wind carried the spores to a larger surrounding area and more than 20,000 people were infected.

of the blood samples resemble common soil bacteria that do not cause disease. Some patients die, even previously healthy young people. The health department calls the Centers for Disease Control and Prevention (CDC) in Atlanta, Georgia, to investigate the illness (Figure 1.2). By midnight 1,200 people are ill and 80 people have died.

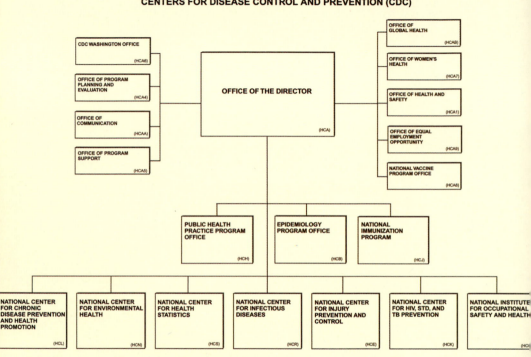

DEPARTMENT OF HEALTH AND HUMAN SERVICES
PUBLIC HEALTH SERVICE

CENTERS FOR DISEASE CONTROL AND PREVENTION (CDC)

Figure 1.2 The Centers for Disease Control and Prevention (CDC), located in Atlanta, Georgia, is a government agency devoted to the health and safety of the public. This organization collects data on outbreaks and epidemics, publishes weekly reports on morbidity and mortality (death and disease), oversees the safety of vaccines, and prepares to deal with any health related issue that might arise. Pictured above is a chart of the CDC's organizational structure showing some of the departments under the auspices of the Public Health Service.

INVESTIGATION

November 5: Morning news reports describe the outbreak. Experts speculate that it might be the Spanish flu, which killed millions in 1918. Others believe that it might be Hong Kong bird flu, which spread from chickens to kill six people in 1997.

The number of people with respiratory symptoms has doubled. Sick and dying people fill health care facilities.

At noon, representatives of health-care and government agencies meet in Northeast. They decide to isolate people with flu-like symptoms and begin interviewing patients and their families to determine the source of the illness. Patients are dying in spite of intensive care. Their symptoms include fever, low blood pressure, and "blood poisoning." Some have meningitis, an infection of the central nervous system. Isolating patients is

THE CDC

The Centers for Disease Control and Prevention is part of the United States Public Health Service. It was established as the Communicable Disease Center in 1946 to work with state and local health departments to fight infectious disease outbreaks. The Epidemic Intelligence Service (EIS) was established in 1951 to send teams to investigate disease outbreaks anywhere in the world.

The mission of the CDC is "to promote health and quality of life by preventing and controlling disease, injury, and disability."[2] The CDC employs about 8,500 people in 170 different areas of public health. Many work at the CDC headquarters in Atlanta, Georgia, but over 2,000 work in other states and 45 countries.

The CDC works with local health departments to detect, diagnose, and contain outbreaks of infectious disease. The CDC also collects health statistics. Each week its *Morbidity and Mortality Weekly Report* (MMWR) publishes the number of people who have become ill and died from certain infectious diseases in every state of the Union. The CDC also promotes vaccination and other disease prevention methods. An extensive web site at *http://www.cdc.gov* provides infectious disease information to health-care workers and to the public.

2. *http://www.cdc.gov/aboutcdc.htm*

difficult because so many people are ill. Hospital staffs begin wearing protective clothing because they are afraid they will become ill. There are not enough protective suits to go around.

By early evening, a university lab has identified the bacteria in several blood samples as the one that causes anthrax (Figure 1.3). The university notifies the state health department, the CDC, and the FBI. Samples are sent to the United States Army Medical Research Institute for Infectious Disease (USAMRIID), which confirms the diagnosis.

The mayor has learned that the FBI had received threats of an anthrax attack but did not warn the city. She is angry that so many people died before the disease was diagnosed. An anthrax vaccine exists, but supplies are low and usually reserved for military personnel.

CAN WE CATCH THE FLU FROM CHICKENS?

Influenza (flu) is a seasonal respiratory disease caused by the influenza virus. In general, most people who get the flu recover with bed rest and fluids. People with weakened immune systems from advanced age or other diseases are at higher risk of dying from influenza.

The influenza virus is constantly mutating; each mutation looks different to the immune system. That is why a new flu vaccine must be developed each year. Occasionally influenza makes such a big change in its appearance that no one is immune, and millions of people worldwide contract influenza.

One of the deadliest **pandemics** (a worldwide disease outbreak) in recorded history was the Spanish flu epidemic in 1918. The epidemic probably began in China. Thousands of soldiers returning from World War I service in Europe brought Spanish flu to the United States The 1918 outbreak was unusual because the flu killed many children and young adults. Six hundred thousand people in the United States and 25 million worldwide died from Spanish flu.

Antibiotics are prescribed for ill and exposed people, but local pharmacies have limited supplies. The total number of people who must be treated is not known. It is known that many (but not all) people who are ill attended the football game on November 1. One expert recommends not treating critically ill people. He says they will die anyway and antibiotics should be saved for those who have a chance of surviving. The mayor requests antibiotics from other states and the federal government.

On TV during the evening news, the mayor announces that anthrax is not contagious. She urges everyone who attended the football game to come to antibiotic distribution centers for a week's supply of medication.

Birds and pigs also get influenza. Occasionally a bird or swine influenza virus and a human influenza virus will infect the same cell, producing a hybrid virus to which most humans have no immunity. Co-infection with bird or swine flu and human flu occurs most often where those animals and humans live closely together. In parts of Asia, chickens, ducks, and pigs commonly live under human dwellings.

Because of the 1918 flu pandemic, an outbreak of chicken flu in Hong Kong in 1997 was closely watched by the world public health community. Millions of chickens died or were killed in the outbreak, and six humans also died. Ten percent of chickens in Hong Kong's open meat markets were infected with chicken flu, and ducks and geese also carried the virus. Fortunately, destruction of the chickens halted the epidemic. The virus is not transmitted efficiently from human to human. Millions of chickens also died from chicken flu in Pennsylvania and Mexico in recent years, but no humans died.

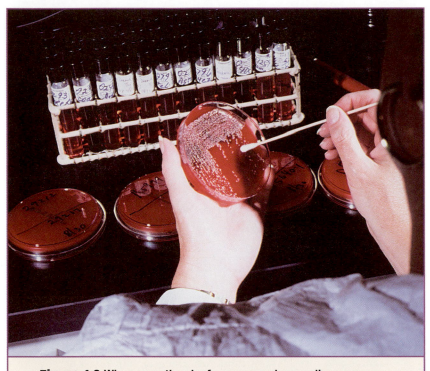

Figure 1.3 When an outbreak of a rare or unknown disease occurs, many government agencies are called to investigate. Identifying the disease and its origin may prove very difficult and involves a lot of research. Samples may be taken from infected patients and grown on special plates so that the microorganism can be studied. The researcher in this picture is cultivating microorganisms on Petri dishes for further analysis.

November 6: By morning, 2,700 people are ill and 300 have died. Schools and homeless shelters become treatment centers. Thousands of people go to doctors' offices and clinics hoping to receive antibiotics. The city has no plan for mass distribution of antibiotics, but several federal agencies are helping. At least 50,000 people receive antibiotics before supplies run out, but no one keeps records of their names. Rumors circulate that antibiotics are being deliberately withheld and that antibiotic distribution centers have been attacked by mobs.

Computer models and interviews with patients show that anthrax has spread eight miles east and one mile north and south of the stadium. No more antibiotics have arrived, although the federal government is promising some by 6:00 P.M. Traffic is jammed; anyone who can tries to leave the city. Some airplane pilots refuse to fly to Northeast, fearing they will become ill. Bus and train service is limited. By midnight 3,200 people are ill and 900 of those have died.

November 7: Antibiotics arrive overnight from the federal government and 40 distribution centers are set up. National Guard troops are stationed at the centers to prevent violence.

The morgues are full of dead bodies, which the CDC says must be cremated to avoid spreading anthrax. Some religious groups protest that their faith does not permit cremation. They threaten to hold private funerals and not report deaths.

Families of the dead are threatening to sue the FBI for not

USAMRIID

The United States Army Medical Research Institute of Infectious Diseases (USAMRIID) is the top Department of Defense lab for biological warfare defense. It is located at Fort Detrick, Maryland, about 50 miles from Baltimore and Washington, D.C. and 20 miles from the Camp David presidential retreat.

Biological warfare research on anthrax was performed at Fort Detrick during World War II. Researchers are currently working at USAMRIID to develop vaccines, drugs and diagnostic techniques that will protect military and civilian populations from attacks with biological agents like anthrax. USAMRIID also trains people to deal with biological attacks and works with the CDC and other agencies worldwide to protect people from biological attacks. Read more at *http://www.usamriid.army.mil/*

issuing warnings and the local government for not having enough antibiotics on hand to treat everyone. No one has claimed responsibility for the attack. By nightfall, 4,000 people are ill and 1,000 have died.

November 8: Many city workers are absent from their jobs. Some are ill or have died. Others have left town to escape becoming ill. Public transport barely runs. Government buildings, schools, and the university are closed. Fire, police, and ambulance responses to emergency calls are slow. Looting breaks out. The mayor holds a press conference to deny rumors that city officials are getting the vaccine while the general public is not. By evening, 4,800 people are ill and 2,400 have died.

AFTERMATH

Of the 20,000 people who were infected, 4,000 died. Most deaths occurred in the first ten days after the attack. Some deaths occurred in other states and a few in other countries, as infected people traveled out of the immediate area. Other people died after stopping antibiotic treatment before the recommended 60 days had passed. More than 250,000 people received antibiotic treatment. Many of these suffered nausea or diarrhea caused by the antibiotics.

Newspapers and television report that many deaths were caused by delays in distributing antibiotics. Some charge that the government was reluctant to spend the $100 per person for the required antibiotics. So far, the FBI has no leads to the people who released the anthrax, although the investigation continues.

The stadium has been abandoned, and Northeast residents call areas downwind from it "The Dead Zone." People who lived and worked in affected areas have refused to return. They demand government compensation for the loss of their homes and businesses. Tourists no longer travel to Northeast.

The FBI receives a threat that five cities will be attacked with anthrax in the next week.

COULD IT HAPPEN?

Dr. Thomas Inglesby, a physician at The Johns Hopkins University School of Medicine in Baltimore, Maryland, wrote the story of Northeast. Baltimore is the model for "Northeast." It has a large, downtown football stadium not far from an elevated stretch of Interstate Highway 95. "Anthrax: A Possible Case History" was published in the CDC journal *Emerging Infectious Diseases* in August, 1999. It was written to show what the consequences of a large-scale anthrax attack on a large United States city would be and to encourage the government to be prepared for such an attack.

In September and October, 2001, more limited attacks did occur on the East Coast of the United States using the mail to carry anthrax.

ANTHRAX PREPAREDNESS IN 1999

In the same issue of *Emerging Infectious Diseases* that carried Thomas Inglesby's anthrax scenario, another physician from The Johns Hopkins School of Medicine in Baltimore, Maryland, expressed concerns about the ability of health-care institutions and workers to respond to an anthrax attack. Dr. John Bartlett reported responses he received from emergency room physicians and laboratory workers when he described the symptoms of anthrax or showed them test results from anthrax patients.

An emergency room physician, who had attended a bio-terrorism course, confirmed that a patient arriving with the early symptoms of inhalational (respiratory) anthrax would probably be diagnosed with influenza. An x-ray technician who was shown a chest x-ray from an anthrax patient did not include anthrax in his list of possible diagnoses. A lab technician said that if the bacterium that causes anthrax was found in patient samples, it would probably be disregarded because a closely related bacterium can get into the lab with dust. Clearly, in 1999 most health-care workers were not expecting an anthrax attack.

2

The Fifth Plague

EXODUS 9

Anthrax is an ancient disease. One of the earliest descriptions may be in the Biblical account of the plagues visited on the Egyptians when they refused to release the Israelites.

Then the Lord said to Moses, "Go to Pharaoh and say to him, 'This is what the Lord, the God of the Hebrews, says: "Let my people go, so that they may worship me." If you refuse to let them go and continue to hold them back, the hand of the Lord will bring a terrible plague on your livestock in the field—on your horses and donkeys and camels and on your cattle and sheep and goats. But the Lord will make a distinction between the livestock of Israel and that of Egypt, so that no animal belonging to the Israelites will die.' "

The Lord set a time and said, "Tomorrow the Lord will do this in the land." And the next day the Lord did it: all the livestock of the Egyptians died, but not one animal belonging to the Israelites died. Pharaoh sent men to investigate and found that not even one of the animals of the Israelites had died. Yet his heart was unyielding and he would not let the people go.

Then the Lord said to Moses and Aaron, "Take handfuls of soot from a furnace and have Moses toss it into the air in the presence of Pharaoh. It will become fine dust over the whole land of Egypt, and festering boils will break out on men and animals throughout the land."

So they took soot from a furnace and stood before Pharaoh. Moses tossed it into the air, and festering boils broke out on men and animals. The magicians could not stand before Moses because of the boils that were on them and on all the Egyptians. But the Lord hardened Pharaoh's heart and he would not listen to Moses and Aaron, just as the Lord had said to Moses.[3]

Anthrax is primarily a disease of hoofed animals: cattle, sheep, goats, camels, and antelopes. The most common form of anthrax in humans appears as black sores on the skin of people who come in contact with infected animals and animal hides. "Anthrax" comes from the Greek word for coal, *anthrakos*. The fifth and sixth plagues of Egypt described in Exodus could be descriptions of animal and human anthrax.

Anthrax is also a key player in two milestones in the field of **microbiology**. Microbiology is the study of bacteria, viruses, and other microscopic organisms, some of which cause disease in humans and animals. In the last third of the nineteenth century, two microbiologists studying anthrax advanced our understanding of infectious disease and how to use vaccination to protect against disease.

ROBERT KOCH CATCHES A GERM

Robert Koch (his last name is pronounced "coke") was a 28-year-old physician in the small German town of Wollstein when his wife gave him a microscope (Figure 2.1). In Wollstein, as in much of Europe, anthrax was killing cows and sheep and occasionally the farmers who tended them. One day the animals would be healthy. The next, they would refuse to eat and their heads would droop. The following day, they would be dead, black blood running from their noses and mouths. Koch knew that in order to cure his human patients, he needed to know what made them sick. In between delivering babies and stitching up farm injuries, he began looking through his

---

3. *Bible*, New International Version, Exodus 9: 1–12.

Figure 2.1 Robert Koch, pictured here, can be considered one of the founding fathers of microbiology. Performing simple experiments where he took blood from anthrax-infected animals and transferred it to healthy animals, he was able to prove that a foreign organism in the blood of the diseased animals was causing the illness. In effect, Koch was the first scientist to prove that a specific microorganism can cause a specific disease.

microscope at the blood from the animals that had died of anthrax, hoping to understand the cause of this disease.

Twenty-five years earlier, in 1849, Aloys Pollender had seen rod-shaped bacteria in the blood of cows that had died of anthrax. Since Anton van Leeuwenhoek, a Dutch lens grinder, first saw bacteria in 1676, several scientists had suggested that bacteria caused disease. However, in 1849 many scientists still

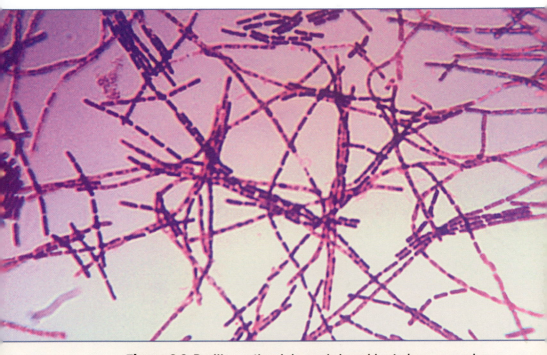

Figure 2.2 *Bacillus anthracis* is a rod-shaped bacterium, as can be seen in this electron micrograph of Gram stained anthrax bacteria. It is generally isolated from blood, skin lesions, or lung fluid of an infected organism. The anthrax bacillus forms spores to protect itself when conditions are unfavorable. Spores have a thick outer coating which shields the bacteria from extreme conditions. When the environment is favorable, the bacteria will shed this outer coating and begin to replicate once again.

thought that bacteria spontaneously appeared in rotting meat and spoiling fruits. They thought bad air or out-of-balance body "humours" caused disease. No one had proved that the rods Pollender saw caused anthrax. Koch set out to obtain that proof.

Koch first used small slivers of wood to inject mice with blood from the spleens of cows that had died of anthrax. As others had shown, mice injected with blood from anthrax-infected cows died, while mice injected with blood from healthy cows remained healthy. The blood of the dead mice contained rods similar to those seen in the blood of the dead cows.

Koch studied the bacteria that cause anthrax, *Bacillus anthracis* <buh-SILL-us an-THRAY-sis>, in his home laboratory. Bacillus anthracis is a rod-shaped bacterium (Figure 2.2). It is a relatively large **bacterium**, one **micron** in diameter by 4–8 microns long (a micron is a millionth of a meter). A human hair is 75–100 microns wide.

Koch grew *Bacillus anthracis* in ox eyes where no other bacteria were present, a technique called **pure culture**. Under the microscope, Koch saw the rods elongate and divide into

BACTERIA

Bacteria are one-celled organisms that are about one-tenth the diameter of most cells in our bodies. Some bacteria live free in soil and water. Others live in or on humans, animals, or plants without causing harm. Some bacteria live in a cooperative arrangement with their plant or animal host, where each provides benefits to the other. Finally, some bacteria cause disease in humans, animals, or plants; they are called **pathogens** <PATH-oh-jens>.

Bacteria, like plants and animals, have two-part scientific names. The first name is the genus and the second is the species. The human genus and species name is *Homo sapiens.*

Like our cells, bacterial cells are filled with a gel-like material called the **cytosol** <SITE-oh-soll> and surrounded by a membrane similar to the skin of a balloon. Unlike our cells, bacteria have rigid cell walls outside their membranes. The cell wall gives bacteria their distinctive shapes: spherical, rod-shaped, or spiral. Bacteria each have one circular DNA molecule containing all the cell's genes, instead of having several linear chromosomes like human cells do.

When conditions are favorable—plenty of food and water,

long chains of rods. He also saw round **spores** inside some of the rods, especially when growth conditions were unfavorable. Spores could survive when the rods died, and Koch showed that when growth conditions were favorable the spores produced new cultures of rods. The new rods could infect and kill mice as well as the original rods isolated from the dead cows. When bacteria were isolated from the newly infected mice, it exactly matched the bacteria that Koch has isolated from anthrax-infected cows. Koch had proved that a single type of bacteria caused anthrax.

Koch's work was published in 1876 and won him recognition as a careful and observant scientist. The conditions he

just the right temperature and humidity—bacteria reproduce by cell division. Each cell grows larger and makes a copy of its DNA. When the cells gets about twice normal size, the membrane pinches off in the middle and new cell wall forms between the two identical **daughter cells**. Each division, which takes from 20 minutes to a few hours, doubles the number of bacteria.

Bacteria are so small that one needs a microscope to see individual cells. One bacterial cell can divide enough times overnight to produce a **colony** of billions of bacteria that can be seen with the naked eye.

Bacteria are one group of **microbes** (microscopic organisms) that cause disease. **Viruses** are much smaller than bacteria and must live inside animal or plant cells, which make millions of virus copies. **Fungi** (molds) usually live in the environment, but occasionally they can infect animals or plants. **Protozoan** <pro-toe-ZO-an> **parasites** can also infect humans. Protozoa are single-celled organisms that have a true nucleus like human cells. The amebas, Euglena, or Paramecium that you may have studied in biology class are protozoa.

developed for growth of bacteria in pure culture led to the formulation of Koch's postulates, rules for the proof that a given bacterium causes a particular infectious disease (see box below).

LOUIS PASTEUR MAKES A WAGER

Louis Pasteur was a French chemist who began his micro-biology career studying "diseases" of the brewing industry (see box on page 26). By 1881, Pasteur was developing vaccines to protect livestock from disease. His first success was with fowl cholera, a disease that was fatal in chickens. When Pasteur and his assistants injected chickens with fresh cultures of the fowl cholera bacterium, the chickens died overnight. When they used old cultures, the chickens appeared sick but then recovered. The

KOCH'S POSTULATES

Robert Koch went from rural physician in 1876 to a respected Professor of Hygiene at the University of Berlin in 1885 and then Director of the Institute for Infectious Diseases in 1891. He studied cholera <KOLL-er-ah> in Egypt and India and rinderpest, malaria, blackwater fever, and plague in Africa.

Koch published methods for culturing bacteria on solid **growth media** so they could easily be separated from other bacteria for study. He demonstrated how to stain bacteria so they were easier to observe under the microscope. He isolated and identified several bacteria, including the one that causes tuberculosis. His studies on cholera led to rules for the control of water-borne diseases. Koch received the Nobel Prize in Physiology or Medicine in 1905.

Although anthrax was the first infectious disease for which Koch demonstrated a bacterial **etiology** <ee-tee-OL-oh-gee> (cause), he published his steps for proving that a particular bacterium caused a particular disease in an 1884 paper report-ing the etiology of tuberculosis. These steps, or postulates, have become the current standards for proving that a microbe fowl cholera bacteria in the old cultures had been **attenuated**, weakened so they could not cause disease. The story goes that Pasteur's lab was short of chickens for his experiments, so they used the chickens that had recovered from the fowl cholera they got from the attenuated cultures. When these chickens were injected with fresh cultures, they did not die but remained perfectly healthy. Pasteur had discovered a way to protect chickens from fowl cholera. He called the process "vaccination", in honor of Edward Jenner's work a century earlier using cowpox to vaccinate people against smallpox. *Vacca* is the Latin word for cow.

Soon Pasteur and his assistants worked out a procedure for attenuating *Bacillus anthracis*. They used the attenuated

---

causes a disease. To satisfy Koch's postulates, one must complete the following four steps:

1. Isolate a bacterium from a person or animal that has died of disease.

2. Grow the bacterium in pure culture in the laboratory.

3. Infect another animal with the bacterium and observe the same disease as in the original person or animal.

4. Isolate the same bacterium from the second animal as from the first.

Koch's postulates have been satisfied for many infectious diseases. However, for other infections the postulates have been impossible to fulfill completely. Viruses must grow inside living cells and cannot be grown in pure culture. Some diseases occur only in humans, so the isolated microbe cannot be used to cause disease in a laboratory animal. Some microbes cause more than one disease: for example, Staphylococcus aureus <STAPH-ul-oh-cock-us ORE-ee-us> causes skin abscesses, food poisoning, and toxic shock syndrome.

anthrax bacteria to inject sheep. The sheep became a little ill but recovered. The sheep were now immune to virulent [VEER-you-lent], disease-causing anthrax bacteria.

When Pasteur announced he had a vaccine for "charbon," as anthrax was called in France, a well-known veterinarian named Monsieur Rossignol challenged him to prove his claims publicly. Monsieur Rossignol was skeptical about the theory that germs caused disease and did not believe Pasteur's claim of a vaccine. At the Agricultural Society of Melun, Rossignol suggested that Pasteur should prove his claims in a large public experiment. The Society collected money to buy 48 sheep, two

"SICK" WINE AND THE DEATH OF SPONTANEOUS GENERATION

In 1856, Louis Pasteur was Professor of Chemistry at The Faculty of Science in Lille, France, when the father of one of his students approached him. Monsieur Bigot had a problem in his distillery, where he produced alcohol from beet root sugar. In some of his vats, no alcohol was produced. The beet sugar mixture turned gray and slimy and became acidic. The distillery was losing money because the contents of the "sick" vats had to be thrown away.

Pasteur took samples from the sick vats and from those that were producing alcohol and studied them under his microscope. The alcohol-producing vats were full of round plump yeasts that had been observed in beer by another Frenchman, Cagniard de le Tour. However, in the sick vats, much smaller rods outnumbered the yeasts. Pasteur concluded that the rods were living bacteria that were producing lactic acid from the beet sugar instead of alcohol. Both alcohol and lactic acid are waste products that result from the chemical breakdown of sugar by the yeasts or bacteria. The process of breaking down the beet sugar to get energy for growth is called *fermentation*.

goats, and several cows for the test. Although Pasteur had only tested his vaccine on sheep in the laboratory, he accepted the challenge. "What worked with fourteen sheep in our laboratory will work with fifty at Melun!"[4] Pasteur is reported to have said. The test was conducted at Pouilly-Le-Fort, a small town outside Paris.

In May 1881, 24 sheep, one goat, and several cows were injected with Pasteur's charbon vaccine. They received a

---

4. David V. Cohn. "The Life and Times of Louis Pasteur" Lecture at University of Louisville Schools of Medicine and Dentistry, Feb. 11, 1996.

Pasteur served as a consultant to the wine and beer industries for many years. His major contribution, however, came from experiments in which he demonstrated conclusively that it was microbes breaking down the sugar in grapes (or beets) that produced alcohol (or lactic acid) and that these microbes were produced from parent microbes.

Other scientists from his time still believed in the **spontaneous generation** of living things from inanimate (non-living) matter. Pasteur grew microbes (microscopic organisms) in broths that were made from inorganic (non-living) materials. He demonstrated that if he heated the broth, no microbes grew. When he allowed dust to enter the flask, microbes appeared. His most elegant apparatus was a flask with a long neck like a swan's. Air could enter through this bent neck, but the broth remained clear of microbes, which were trapped in the bend of the neck. If the broth were allowed to flow into the bend of the neck and come in contact with the dust trapped there, microbes quickly appeared in the broth. Even microbes must have parents!

second vaccination two weeks later with a slightly stronger vaccine. On May 31, Pasteur injected all the vaccinated and unvaccinated animals with virulent *Bacillus anthracis*. Interested observers, including a reporter from London, gathered to learn the results. Within two days, all the unvaccinated animals died of anthrax, while all vaccinated animals survived. Pasteur had won his wager (Figure 2.3).

The experiment was widely reported, and Pasteur received requests for the vaccine from across Europe. All was not smooth sailing, however. Preparing the vaccine under the primitive conditions in Pasteur's lab was difficult. His assistants worked overtime to produce enough doses. Some doses were contaminated with other bacteria, while others were not sufficiently attenuated. Although the vaccine protected many animals from anthrax, many other vaccinated animals died. Typically, for he was not as methodical as Koch was, Pasteur ignored the failures and pressed forward with his vaccine work. He went on to develop the first rabies vaccine.

ANIMAL ANTHRAX IN MODERN TIMES

A farmer goes out to check on his cattle or sheep and finds one or several dead. The bodies are bloated and still bleeding from the nose, mouth, and rectum. The animals may have seemed perfectly healthy the previous day, or they may have appeared somewhat drowsy or uninterested in food. Today, though, they are dead. This scenario is typical of anthrax.

Anthrax is primarily a disease of herbivores, animals that graze for food, such as cattle, sheep, goats, camels, and antelopes. Pigs are somewhat susceptible, while birds are rarely infected. Eating meat contaminated with anthrax spores may infect cats and dogs. These animals often recover from the disease without treatment. Not all infected animals, even herbivores, die from anthrax. Whether the animal survives or dies probably depends on the dose of spores and the natural immunity of the animal.

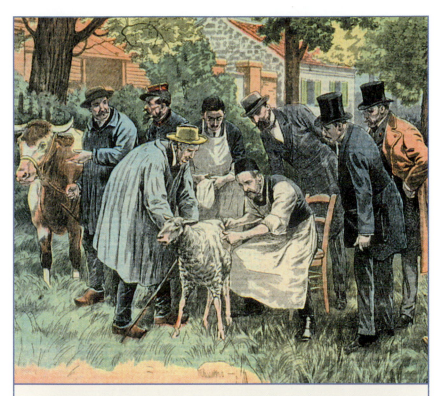

Figure 2.3 Louis Pasteur created the first version of the anthrax vaccination for animals. He found that using a weakened version of the anthrax bacteria caused animals to get sick, but then to recover. When these animals were later injected with a stronger version of the anthrax bacteria, they remained healthy. In the historical painting above, Louis Pasteur demonstrates his anthrax vaccine to a group of onlookers.

As blood flows from an animal dying of anthrax, the bacteria in the blood quickly form spores to protect themselves from the harsh environment in the soil. **Spores** are anthrax bacteria in a state of suspended animation, protected by a thick coat from drying out. Animals that die from anthrax leave spores in the soil. Decades later, anthrax can still infect other animals that ingest or inhale the spores as they graze. Runoff from sewage or a nearby tanning plant may also carry spores

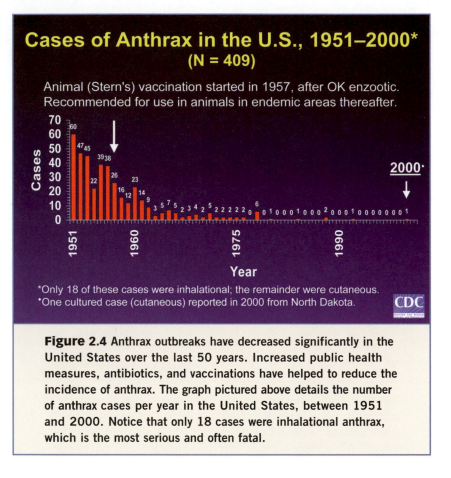

Figure 2.4 Anthrax outbreaks have decreased significantly in the United States over the last 50 years. Increased public health measures, antibiotics, and vaccinations have helped to reduce the incidence of anthrax. The graph pictured above details the number of anthrax cases per year in the United States, between 1951 and 2000. Notice that only 18 cases were inhalational anthrax, which is the most serious and often fatal.

into the field. Feeding carcasses of infected animals to other animals also spreads anthrax.

The farmer may have noticed that the animal had a fever, its breathing was labored, it was not hungry, it was not giving as much milk as usual, it had difficulty walking, or it had convulsions. The disease can cause death so quickly, however, that the farmer may have seen no signs of illness before he found his animal dead in the field. Bleeding after death from the nose, mouth, and rectum may be the first signs that the animal died of anthrax. In some locations, biting flies transmit anthrax. If anthrax enters the skin through the bite of an insect, the site of the bite is usually swollen from damage caused by the anthrax bacteria.

Anthrax occurs in countries around the world. The **disease incidence** (number of cases) is decreasing due to improved public health measures and vaccination (Figure 2.4). Risk is highest in temperate agricultural areas: Central and South America, southern Europe, equatorial Africa, and parts of Asia. The disease is sporadic in Australia. In Canada, anthrax occurred most recently in wood bison in northern Alberta. In the United States, anthrax outbreaks occur periodically in Texas, Oklahoma, Nebraska, and South Dakota along the route of cattle drives in the 1800s. Periods of drought followed by heavy rains seem to favor disease outbreaks.

When outbreaks of anthrax occur, animals are vaccinated and treated with antibiotics. Carcasses of dead animals must be burned to prevent spore transmission to other animals or to humans.

3

Human Anthrax

In August 2000, a North Dakota farmer found five of his cows dead of anthrax. Wearing leather gloves, he carefully placed chains around the heads and hooves of the dead cows and moved them to a burial site.

Four days later, he noticed a small bump on his left cheek. When he went to the doctor two days later, the bump was the size of a quarter and was covered with a black scab. The bump was firm but not painful and was surrounded by a purple ring. The farmer had no fever or other symptoms. He was treated with antibiotics for two weeks. The bump on his face improved slowly and eventually disappeared. The farmer's blood tested positive for antibodies to anthrax.

During the 2000 anthrax outbreak, 157 animals died on 31 North Dakota farms. Sixty-two people, including farmers, veterinarians, and laboratory technicians, were in contact with those animals or their tissues. Only one developed anthrax.

Anthrax is a **zoonosis** <zoo-oh-NO-sis>, which means it is an infectious disease that can be transmitted from animals to humans under natural conditions. Most human cases of anthrax occur in people who have repeated contact with cattle, sheep, or goats, or with hides or hair from infected animals. Eating infected meat is another source of human infection. Direct human-to-human spread of anthrax does not occur. Human anthrax infections occur in three forms: skin (cutaneous), digestive (gastrointestinal), and respiratory (inhalational).

CUTANEOUS ANTHRAX

Worldwide, 95 percent of human anthrax cases are **cutaneous** <cue-TANE-ee-us>, or skin infections. Between 1955 and 2000, 203 human

ZOONOSES

Over 200 diseases can spread from animals to humans. Some spread only between humans and other primates. In 1998, a worker at a primate research center died from a Herpes B virus infection contracted from a rhesus macaque. Infected material from the macaque, which did not appear ill, was splashed in the worker's eye as she was working outside its cage.

Bacillus anthracis is one of the infectious organisms that can cause disease in both humans and more distantly related animals. Some zoonotic <zoo-oh-NOT-ik> microbes are spread from the digestive tract of animals to the digestive tract of humans by means of contaminated food or water. These include the bacteria *Escherichia coli* 0157, Salmonella, and Listeria, and the parasites Giardia <gee-ARE-dee-ah> and Cryptosporidium <crypto-spore-ID-ee-um>, all of which cause vomiting and diarrhea. Tuberculosis can be transmitted from cows to humans in milk from infected cows. If a pregnant woman changes the litter box of a cat infected with the parasite Toxoplasma (which the cat acquired from eating infected wild animals) and does not wash her hands thoroughly, she may become infected. The Toxoplasma parasite can cross the placenta and cause serious birth defects in her unborn child.

Many other diseases can also be transmitted from animals to humans. Hantavirus can be transmitted from mice to humans in inhaled dust contaminated with dried urine. Rabies virus is transmitted by an animal bite. Lyme disease is a bacterial disease transmitted from the normal host, white tailed deer, to humans by the bite of a tick. Ticks also transmit bubonic plague and typhus from animals to humans.

Los Angeles County has an excellent web site on zoonoses at *http://phps2.dhs.co.la.ca.us/vet/guides/vetzooman.htm*.

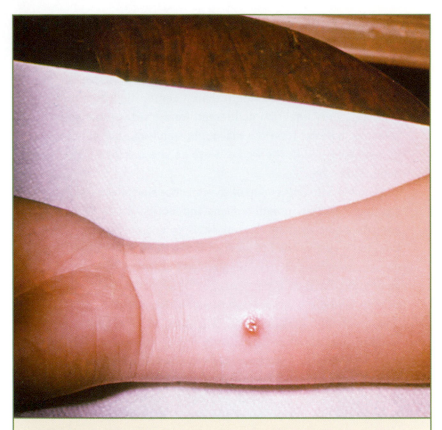

Figure 3.1 Cutaneous anthrax, the most common form of the disease, is usually not lethal. People can become infected by having a lot of contact with infected animals or contaminated soil. At first, a small bump may form at the site of infection, followed by a black scab. Cutaneous anthrax can be treated with antibiotics, and patients usually recover fully.

anthrax cases were recorded in the United States. The case of the North Dakota farmer in 2000 was the first since 1992. Most United States cases are also cutaneous.

Anthrax spores from the soil or from the hides of infected animals enter human tissues through a break in the skin, usually on the hands, forearms, or face. After a few days, a small, painless bump appears at the infection site (Figure 3.1).

Figure 3.2 In the photo above, a textile worker in Memphis, Tennessee, processes raw materials. Anthrax spores may be transmitted to humans through animal hide or hair. Spores that lie dormant in the animal hair can enter the human body though cuts or small openings on the face, hands, or arms. This is how the North Carolina man, in the scenario described in the text, contracted the disease. Cutaneous anthrax is usually not fatal.

As the bump grows, a black scab forms in the center. Fever, fatigue, and headache are other symptoms of cutaneous anthrax. The area around the bump and nearby lymph nodes in the armpit or neck may swell.

In July 1987, a North Carolina textile plant worker (Figure 3.2) noticed a small red swollen sore on his right forearm. Over the next week, the sore became full of fluid and covered with a black scab. The man visited his doctor and began antibiotic therapy. The next day he was admitted to the hospital with fever, chills, and pain and swelling in his arm. He was diagnosed with cutaneous anthrax and given **intravenous** <intra-VEEN-us> antibiotics. He recovered and returned to work in late August. No anthrax bacteria could be isolated from his blood or wound tissue, but his blood did contain antibodies to anthrax.

The man had not traveled out of state or been exposed to wild or domestic animals. The textile mill where he worked produced yarn from United States, Australian, and New Zealand wool, Cashmere goat hair from China, Afghanistan, and Iran, and camel hair from China and Mongolia. This was the first case of anthrax in the 25-year history of the mill. None of the other 210 workers at the mill developed anthrax.

Bacillus anthracis was isolated from five samples of West Asian cashmere, one sample of Australian wool, and two samples of debris from the mill. Fifty-one other samples from the mill were negative for anthrax bacteria. *Bacillus anthracis* was also found in eight of 12 cashmere samples from the plant in Texas where the imported wool was washed before being shipped to North Carolina. The worker was almost certainly infected by contact with anthrax spores on the imported goat hair. The CDC recommended vaccination programs for employees at both the North Carolina and Texas plants.

People of all ages appear equally susceptible to cutaneous anthrax. However, since most exposures are work-related, most cases in the United States occur in adults. Notice that in both cases many more people were exposed to anthrax than became ill.

Cutaneous anthrax is not usually fatal. Even without antibiotic treatment, 80 percent of infected people will recover. Antibiotic treatment for one to two weeks cures over

99 percent of people with cutaneous anthrax. Rarely, anthrax spreads from the skin to the brain to cause anthrax **meningitis** <men-in-JITE-us>, an infection of the membranes covering the brain and spinal cord. Fever, fatigue, nausea and vomiting, headache, and a stiff neck are symptoms of anthrax meningitis. Agitation, seizures, and delirium may also occur. Anthrax meningitis is usually fatal even with antibiotic treatment.

GASTROINTESTINAL ANTHRAX

In July 2000, a Minnesota farmer had a cow that was unable to stand. The local veterinarian decided it was safe to eat meat from the cow, so the farmer butchered it and took the carcass to a private meat processing plant. Five family members ate hamburger or steak from the carcass. One had diarrhea that lasted one day, beginning about two days after eating meat from the cow. Another family member had abdominal pain, diarrhea, and a fever of 102°F (39°C) that began one to two days after eating the meat and lasted three days. Both recovered without any treatment.

In late August 2000, the same farmer found five of his cattle dead in his pasture. The cattle were tested for anthrax and *Bacillus anthracis* was isolated from one of them. When the Minnesota Department of Health interviewed the family, they learned of the earlier illnesses. Tests of meat from the ill cow showed high levels of anthrax bacteria in the carcass. Because the family had been exposed to infected meat, they were vaccinated against anthrax and treated with antibiotics.

Anthrax spores can enter small openings anywhere in mucus membranes lining the mouth and digestive tract (Figure 3.3). When infection occurs in the mouth or throat, swelling and sores are visible. When infection occurs further down the digestive tract, symptoms include fever, abdominal pain, vomiting, and diarrhea. Blood may be vomited or appear in the stool.

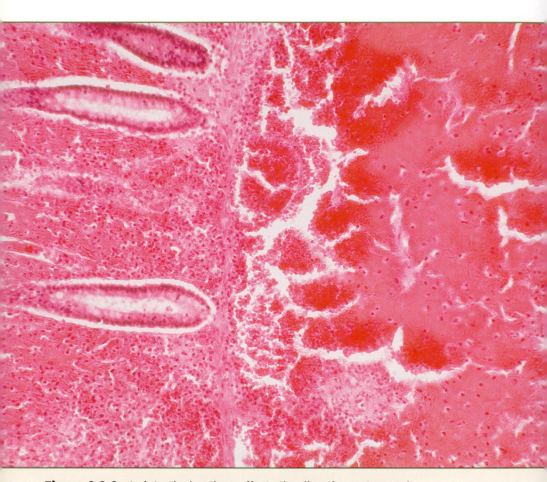

Figure 3.3 Gastrointestinal anthrax affects the digestive system and can lead to diarrhea, upset stomach, and sores and swelling of the mouth and throat. Anthrax spores can enter the body via mucous membranes that line the mouth and intestines. Humans can also contract gastro-intestinal anthrax by eating meat from an infected animal. The large intestine pictured here has begun to hemorrhage due to the presence of anthrax bacilli.

Gastrointestinal anthrax is very rare in the United States because animals are vaccinated against anthrax and meat is inspected and well cooked before being eaten. In the Minnesota case from 2000, even though the meat had anthrax bacteria, the family members may have gotten diarrhea from other bacteria that can cause intestinal illnesses.

In countries where animal anthrax is more common, gastrointestinal anthrax probably occurs more often. Poor people in rural areas eat meat from sick or dead animals because that is all that is available. In addition, because gastrointestinal illness is so common and access to medical care is difficult, gastrointestinal anthrax is never diagnosed in many people who get it. Anywhere from 10–50 percent of people with gastrointestinal anthrax will die if not treated with antibiotics.

INHALATIONAL ANTHRAX

On September 24, 2001, a mailroom clerk at a Florida newspaper began to feel very tired. Within a few days he had a runny nose, a nonproductive cough, inflamed eyes, and a fever. His condition worsened and he was admitted to the hospital on October 1. He developed pneumonia and was treated with antibiotics. *Bacillus anthracis* was found in his lungs. The mailroom clerk became a survivor of the first bioterrorist anthrax attack in the United States.

When anthrax spores enter the body through the lungs, the disease is called inhalational anthrax. In the 1800s, inhalational anthrax was called **woolsorter's disease** in England and **ragpicker's disease** in Germany and Austria because workers in the textile industry contracted the disease from spores on animal fibers. Workers in the American textile and tanning industries were at risk for inhalational anthrax during the early 1900s. Before the bioterrorist attacks in 2001, the most recent case of inhalational anthrax in the United States occurred in 1976.

Inhalational anthrax begins as a typical upper respiratory illness. Sufferers develop fever, **nonproductive cough** (nothing coughed up), muscle pain, and fatigue, just as they would if they were coming down with the flu. The illness quickly

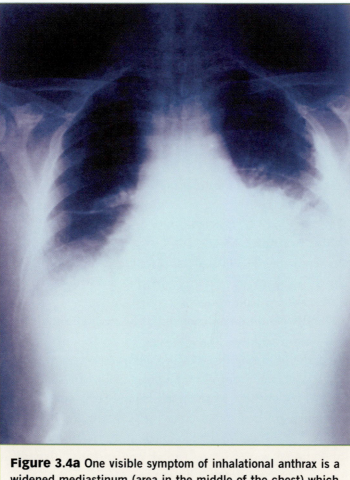

Figure 3.4a One visible symptom of inhalational anthrax is a widened mediastinum (area in the middle of the chest) which can be seen on the X-ray photograph above (a). Figure 3.4b is a normal chest X-ray. Notice that the mediastinum is much smaller. Antibiotics are often ineffective on inhalational anthrax, which is the most deadly form of anthrax.

becomes much worse. The lymph nodes in the **mediastinum**, the middle of the chest (Figures 3.4a and 3.4b), become swollen with *Bacillus anthracis* and white blood cells trying to fight the infection. The lungs fill with fluid and blood pressure drops.

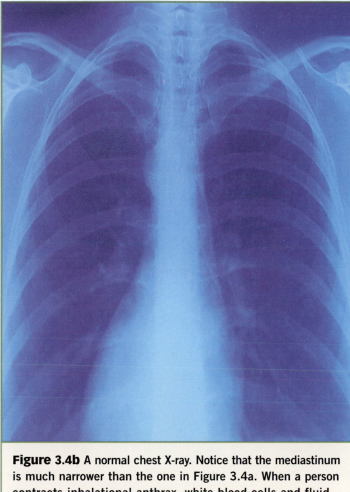

Figure 3.4b A normal chest X-ray. Notice that the mediastinum is much narrower than the one in Figure 3.4a. When a person contracts inhalational anthrax, white blood cells and fluid collect in this area of the chest, in an attempt to fight the disease, causing the mediastinum to appear much larger in a chest X-ray.

Inhalational anthrax is the most deadly form of anthrax. Even with antibiotic treatment, most patients die. Survival of six out of the first ten people who developed inhalational anthrax in the 2001 bioterrorist attacks was much higher than what was predicted.

4

How Anthrax Causes Disease

Pathogens (disease-causing microbes) cause illness in several ways. One method is for the pathogens to hide from the immune system, so that they are not killed before they can reproduce and spread to another **host** (the infected human or animal). Another way is to damage host cells, either by invading the cells or by making toxins that damage them. The third way is by activating the **immune system**. The powerful signals the immune system sends in an attempt to remove the pathogen can also make us sick as well as help us. If the immune signals are unsuccessful, they can actually damage the body they were designed to protect. All of these **virulence** (<VEER-you-lance>, disease-causing) factors are used by *Bacillus anthracis.*

RESERVOIRS

Just as a water reservoir stores water for later use, a **disease reservoir** contains infectious organisms between disease outbreaks. For anthrax, the disease reservoir is spores that remain in suspended animation in the soil, ready to become living, disease-causing bacteria when they enter an animal or human.

When an animal dies of anthrax, its blood is full of *Bacillus anthracis.* As many as ten million to 100 million bacterial cells can be present in one milliliter of blood, about a fifth of a teaspoon. The anthrax toxin keeps blood from clotting, so after death blood spills onto the ground from body openings. When *Bacillus anthracis* comes in contact with the oxygen in the air, each cell rapidly forms a spore. Spores have very thick coats so they can resist drying, and their DNA is protected from damage by UV radiation (Figure 4.1). Spores may lie dormant in soil more for than 100 years and still be able to infect animals or humans. *Bacillus anthracis* could not survive outside of an animal or human without the ability to form spores. It is an

DISEASE RESERVOIRS

Any disease that is not constantly causing human infections must have a reservoir from which it can spread during disease outbreaks. **Disease reservoirs** include soil and water, animals, and humans who have no disease symptoms.

The bacteria that cause tetanus usually live in the soil and only infect humans when the bacteria accidentally enter deep wounds. Organisms that cause diarrhea can often survive for some time in water that is contaminated with feces from an infected animal or human.

Infected animals provide reservoirs for many diseases that occasionally infect humans. Examples include cattle and sheep for anthrax, prairie dogs for plague, mice for Hantavirus, deer for Lyme disease, and birds for West Nile virus.

Some microbes have human reservoirs. Cold and influenza viruses travel from human to human. Outbreaks occur more often in winter, but someone is always ill with these viruses. Some people can be infected but not show symptoms; these people are disease **carriers**. A famous carrier was Typhoid Mary. She was infected with the bacterium that causes typhoid and spread it to the families she worked for as a cook.

Many bacteria live on and in our bodies all the time as **normal flora**. Normal flora block attachment by pathogens and supply us with vitamins. However, if they enter our tissues in a wound or surgical incision they can cause serious disease. These organisms are called **opportunistic pathogens** since they only cause disease when the opportunity to enter the body occurs.

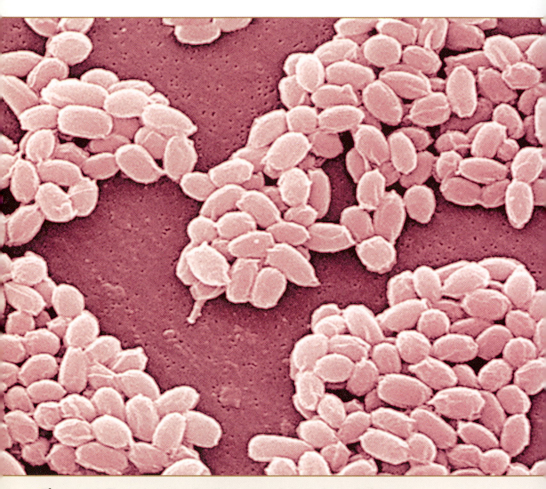

Figure 4.1 The rod-shaped *Bacillus anthracis* bacterium will form an oval-shaped spore (thick outer coating) to protect it from harsh conditions when the environment is not ideal for replication. Anthrax spores can live for more than 100 years! This electron micrograph shows what the bacteria look like when they form spores.

obligate pathogen, a bacterium that must live inside an animal or human to survive.

Anthrax spores survive in the environment until they are eaten along with grass by a host animal. Anthrax seems to appear in times of drought, perhaps because the dry vegetation is more likely to scratch the animal's digestive tract and cause openings that allow the spores to enter the body. Heavy rains after a drought can concentrate the spores in low areas. When animals become infected and die, more spores are deposited in the soil. Humans almost always become infected from spores on the coats or in the meat from infected animals.

SPORES

Spores are cells in suspended animation, not growing or dividing. They are covered by a thick coat that protects them from extreme temperatures, drying, or UV radiation. Bacteria form spores when conditions are unfavorable for survival. Two groups of pathogenic bacteria, Bacillus and Clostridium <claus-TRIH-dee-um>, can make spores. Clostridia live in the soil, but if they get into wounds or food they can cause tetanus, botulism, food poisoning, and gas gangrene. Molds and mushrooms (fungi) also form spores when they reproduce.

Bacteria make spores when food is scarce, their environment becomes too hot or too dry, or when oxygen levels increase. First, each growing bacterial cell (the **vegetative** cell) makes a copy of its DNA. Then the bacterial cell membrane pinches off part of the cytosol containing the new DNA until there is a smaller cell inside the vegetative cell. A thick spore coat forms around the smaller cell which becomes the spore. Special proteins in the spore protect its DNA from UV damage and provide nutrients for when the spore is ready to become a vegetative cell again. The old vegetative cell shrivels around the outside of the spore and the spore remains dormant during difficult times.

Germination, or growth of a vegetative cell from a spore, occurs rapidly when conditions become favorable. Germination reverses the process of sporulation. The thick spore coat breaks down, water is absorbed, and the cell swells. The special protective proteins are destroyed. Finally, the cell begins to divide and produce more vegetative cells.

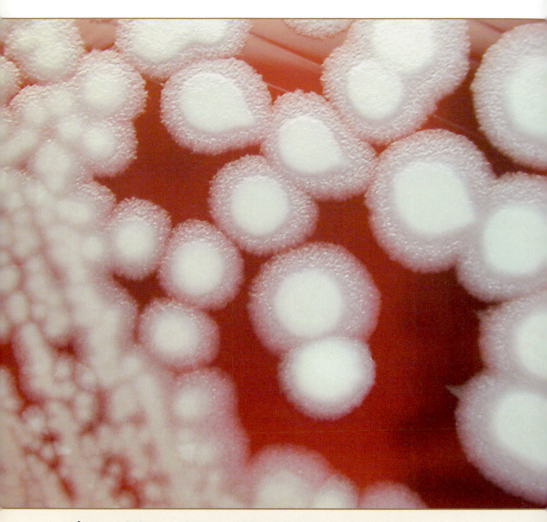

Figure 4.2 When anthrax spores find favorable growth conditions, they will shed their thick outer coating and begin to replicate. In the photo above, anthrax bacteria grow on sheep blood agar.

INFECTION

When the spores enter the body of a human or animal host, they find perfect conditions for growth. Oxygen is low, nutrients are plentiful, and the blood circulation will carry them anywhere in the body. Somehow, the spore can sense that conditions have changed for the better, and it sheds its thick coat and becomes a **vegetative** (actively growing) **cell** (Figure 4.2).

Phagocytes <FAG-oh-sites> are white blood cells whose job it is to engulf and kill pathogens. **Macrophages** (<macro-FAGES> "big eaters") in the skin and lungs, and monocytes and neutrophils in the blood are types of phagocytes. Macrophages are the first line of defense once *Bacillus anthracis* gets past skin and mucus membrane barriers.

Phagocytes recognize microbes by molecules on the microbe's surface that stick to receptors on the outer membrane of the phagocytes. **Receptors** are proteins on cell membranes that bind (stick to) microbes, hormones like insulin, growth factors, or food materials like sugars or amino acids. Receptor binding signals the cell to do something in response: engulf what they have bound, begin dividing, make chemical signals that will bind receptors on other cells, or die. Different types of cells have different receptors, depending on what signals they need to receive. Phagocytes have receptors for molecules commonly found on bacteria.

In response to binding *Bacillus anthracis* to their receptors, phagocytes put out long **pseudopodia** <sude-oh-PODE-ee-ah>, "fingers" of their cell surface, to surround the pathogens (Figure 4.3). When a pathogen is completely surrounded, it is taken inside the phagocyte in a **vesicle** (bubble) surrounded by a membrane. The phagocyte then fills the vesicle with molecules that will kill and digest the pathogen. Some of these molecules are enzymes that destroy bacterial proteins, while others are **superoxides** that inactivate enzymes the bacteria need to grow.

Bacillus anthracis does several things to avoid death by phagocytosis. Spores are naturally resistant to the phagocyte killing molecules just as they are to the harsh environment outside the body. In fact, they can become vegetative cells inside the phagocyte vesicle and begin to divide there. From inside, anthrax bacteria kill the phagocyte and cause it to

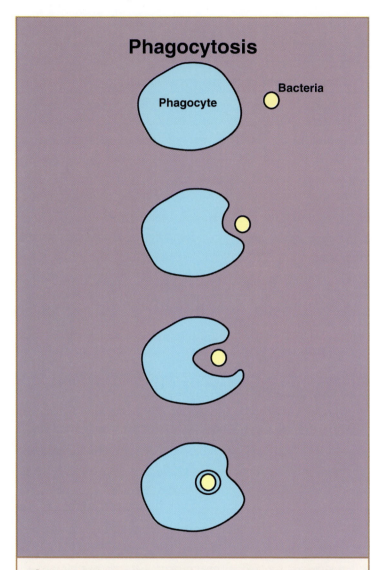

Figure 4.3 Phagocytes are part of the body's defense system. They protect the body from foreign invaders by swallowing the invader whole, in a process called phagocytosis (literally, "cell eating"). As shown in the diagram above, the phagocyte will stretch out "arms" and encircle the invader, drawing it into its interior. Special enzymes inside the phagocyte will then begin to degrade the foreign body.

break open, releasing the bacteria into the tissues. Destructive enzymes and superoxides are also released from the phago-cytes, killing nearby host cells.

Bacillus anthracis may divide at the infection site or be carried to nearby lymph nodes. Lymph nodes are located throughout the body. Their job is to filter pathogens from the fluids that bathe body tissues. Once *Bacillus anthracis* is growing in the skin or lymph nodes near the infection site, it makes a sugary coating called a **capsule** around its cell. Phagocytes cannot stick to capsules the way they can to the bacterial surface, so *Bacillus anthracis* can grow and divide without being engulfed.

Phagocytes that have encountered bacteria send out chemical signals called **cytokines** to attract other phagocytes to their location. Other cytokines make nearby blood vessels leaky, so passing phagocytes can leave the circulation and move into the infection site to help eliminate the bacteria. Blood molecules called **complement** also leak into the infection site; their job is to stick to the bacteria and make them easier for the phagocytes to engulf.

In cutaneous anthrax, phagocytes and fluid leaking into the skin result in the bump at the infection site. Lymph nodes nearby, in the armpit or neck, may also swell from dividing *Bacillus anthracis* and from increased numbers of white blood cells trying to eliminate the bacteria. When *Bacillus anthracis* infects the throat in gastrointestinal anthrax, swelling can be seen in the tonsils, collections of tissue similar to lymph nodes.

At this point in infection, especially in cutaneous anthrax if most of the bacteria are still at the infection site, phagocytes may still be able to engulf and kill all of the bacteria, and the infection will be eliminated without treatment. The black area on the skin, caused by death of phagocytes and surrounding skin cells, will heal as new cells replace the ones that have died.

In inhalational anthrax, *Bacillus anthracis* does not divide in the lung tissue but prefers the nearby **mediastinal**

<media-STINE-al> lymph nodes in the center of the chest. Enlargement of these mediastinal lymph nodes shows up on a chest X-ray and is one of the earliest signs in patients with inhalational anthrax. Lymph nodes contain many macrophages that will be infected and killed by *Bacillus anthracis*. The immune system has lost the battle once *Bacillus anthracis* reaches the mediastinal lymph nodes and from there the blood, and only aggressive antibiotic treatment can save the patient.

TOXINS

Many bacteria damage host cells using proteins called toxins. Toxins released from the bacterial cells are called **exotoxins**. Like anthrax toxin, exotoxins can spread throughout the body to damage cells.

The toxins that cause tetanus and botulism are **neurotoxins**. They interfere with signals from motor neurons to muscle fibers. Botulism is caused by a bacterium that normally lives in the soil, *Clostridium botulinum* <claus-TRIH-dee-um bot-you-LINE-um>. The bacteria usually grow only in the absence of oxygen. If food containing Clostridium is improperly canned, allowing spores to survive, the spores germinate and the vegetative cells produce toxin. Botulism toxin is colorless and odorless and can be destroyed by cooking. It interferes with the nerve signals that cause muscles to contract, so affected muscles remain relaxed and unresponsive. Tetanus is caused by *Clostridium tetani* <claus-TRIH-dee-um TET-an-eye> that enter deep wounds through cuts or punctures. Tetanus toxin interferes with the chemicals that relax muscles, so a person with tetanus develops uncontrolled muscle contraction that could possibly bend him backward into a "U" with his head touching his heels.

Several bacteria make **enterotoxins** that damage the cells of the intestinal lining, causing fluid loss and diarrhea. Diseases caused by enterotoxins include cholera, dysentery,

INTOXICATION

Bacillus anthracis has one more weapon it can deploy to protect itself from the immune system and make sure it is spread to other hosts: toxin production. **Intoxication** is the process whereby toxins enter cells and damage or kill them. Many bacteria produce toxins that cause disease symptoms. *Bacillus anthracis* produces three protein molecules that combine to form two toxins. Once antibiotic treatment has begun

gastroenteritis caused by *E. coli*, and "food poisoning" caused by *Bacillus cereus*, *Clostridium perfringens*, and *Staphylococcus aureus*.

Diphtheria toxin blocks the ability of cells to make proteins. As cells in the throat die from diphtheria toxin and phagocytes enter the area to try to control the damage, the cells form a membrane that blocks breathing. Interestingly, the genes that carry the information to make diphtheria toxin are in a virus that infects diphtheria bacteria. Bacteria not infected by the virus do not make toxin and do not cause diphtheria.

Streptococcus pyogenes <strep-toe-COCK-us pie-AH-jen-ees>, the bacterium that causes "strep throat," produces toxins that cause rashes, break open red blood cells, and make the skin peel. The "flesh-eating" form of *Streptococcus pyogenes* makes a toxin that causes blood to clot, blocking oxygen distribution to the tissues.

Staphylococcus aureus <STAPH-el-oh-cock-us ORE-ee-us> is probably the champion toxin producer. *Staphylococcus aureus* lives harmlessly on the skin of many people, but when it enters the body it causes a variety of diseases. *Staphylococcus aureus* toxins break open red and white blood cells, form clots around the bacteria to hide them from white blood cells, induce vomiting and diarrhea, and cause toxic shock with internal bleeding and low blood pressure.

to kill the bacteria, toxin can even remain in the blood for several days to spread and kill host cells. Macrophages seem to be the prime target of the toxins, weakening the immune defense against the bacteria. The symptoms of anthrax can be induced in animals by giving them toxin in the absence of live bacteria.

Protective Antigen (**PA**) is required for both of the toxins to kill cells. PA binds to the membranes of infected human or animal cells. A host cell enzyme then cuts off the tip of the PA molecule. Seven trimmed PA molecules join to form a round pore in the membrane of the host cell through which the other toxins can enter. Although PA helps the toxins to kill cells, it is called a "protective" antigen because when it is injected into laboratory animals or humans, it acts as a vaccine to protect against future infection with *Bacillus anthracis*.

Lethal Factor (**LF**) is produced by *Bacillus anthracis* in the macrophage vesicle. It attaches to the ring of PA molecules in the vesicle membrane and is carried into the cytosol of the macrophage. This combination of LF and PA is called **Lethal Toxin** (**LeTX**). Once in the cytosol of the macrophage, lethal toxin signals the macrophage to make large amounts of the cytokines that make the blood vessels leaky. So much fluid leaks from the circulation that the host suffers from low blood pressure and shock. This may account for the sudden death often seen in anthrax. Lethal toxin also causes the macrophage to overproduce superoxide. As *Bacillus anthracis* kills the macrophages, superoxide is released to kill nearby host cells. *Bacillus anthracis* released from the dead macrophage can spread and make more lethal toxin, which can enter other macrophages and kill them.

Edema Factor (**EF**) also needs PA in order to enter the host cell cytosol. The combination of EF and PA is called **Edema Toxin** (**EdTx**). **Edema** <eh-DEE-ma> is swelling caused by fluid leaking from the blood circulation into the tissues. Edema toxin interferes with the normal flow of water and salts,

VIRULENCE FACTORS ALLOW *BACILLUS ANTHRACIS* TO SURVIVE INSIDE MACROPHAGES

Scientists have studied what happens when anthrax spores are engulfed by mouse macrophages in the laboratory. In these experiments, macrophages readily engulfed spores of *Bacillus anthracis*. Within three hours, the spores germinated inside macrophage vesicles. *Bacillus anthracis* producing lethal toxin and edema toxin remained alive inside the macrophages and began to disrupt their vesicle membranes.

In contrast, mutant *Bacillus anthracis* that could not make PA, lethal factor, or edema factor were killed during the three-hour experiment and the macrophages remained healthy. These findings suggest that toxin production protects *Bacillus anthracis* from macrophage killing. Once the macrophages die and release *Bacillus anthracis*, the bacterium divides and produces more toxin to kill other cells from the outside.

so that water leaks out of cells. Edema toxin damages blood vessel walls, so fluid leaks into the tissues and causes more swelling. In inhalational anthrax, fluids collecting in and around the lungs due to toxin action interfere with breathing.

Numbers of bacteria and toxin levels increase dramatically in the few hours just before death from anthrax. In these last few hours, *Bacillus anthracis* escapes completely from the control of the immune system and doubles its numbers every one to two hours. Toxin levels increase with the numbers of bacteria. At some point, so many host cells are damaged and shock is so widespread that treatment cannot save the patient.

5

Deadly Letters (Outbreak 2001)

PROLOGUE

Following the September 11, 2001, attacks on the World Trade Center and the Pentagon, a wave of bioterrorism swept over the east coast. Terrorists delivered anthrax spores via letters sent through the mail to several influential people. Not only did the tainted letters cause illness and death, but they lead to nationwide panic. The actions of these terrorists affected more than just their designated targets. What follows is a chronology of the events which comprised the 2001 Anthrax Attacks.

OUTBREAK

September 25: A letter addressed to NBC News anchor Tom Brokaw and postmarked Trenton, New Jersey, arrives at NBC offices in New York City. The envelope contains a white powdery substance. NBC notifies law enforcement agencies and the FBI.

October 1: Erin O'Connor, the 38-year-old assistant to Tom Brokaw who handled the letter, goes to her doctor with a rash. Her doctor notifies the New York City Department of Health, which tests the letter for anthrax. Results are negative.

Ernesto Blanco, a 73-year-old mailroom supervisor at American Media Inc. (AMI) in Boca Raton, Florida is admitted to the hospital. He had complained of fatigue about a week earlier, and four days earlier he developed a nonproductive cough, runny nose, and conjunctivitis, an infection of the membranes surrounding the eye. He had a fever that came and went. Over the next four days, his cough and fatigue worsened. He became short of breath when he exercised and suffered from fever and sweating. He began vomiting. His family and co-workers noticed that he appeared confused at times.

When he was admitted to the hospital, Blanco had a fever and his heart rate and respiratory rate were higher than normal. Both eyes were infected and his lungs were congested. His white blood cell (WBC) count was normal; WBC counts often increase during an infection. Tests showed his blood was carrying less oxygen than normal. He had no skin lesions and was not a smoker. Doctors began antibiotic treatment.

October 2: Robert Stevens, a 63-year-old photo editor at AMI awoke early with nausea, vomiting, and confusion. He had started to feel ill on a trip to North Carolina about five days earlier. His symptoms included fatigue, chills and fever, lack of appetite, and sweating. His family took him to the hospital emergency room (ER).

Stevens had a fever and an elevated heart rate. He did not know his own name, where he was, or what day it was. His WBC count was normal. His chest x-ray showed a widened area at the top of his mediastinum and possible fluid leaking into his left lung. He had bacteria in his spinal fluid, which normally is free of microbes.

October 3: Florida health officials announce that Stevens has inhalational anthrax. The hospital lab isolated *Bacillus anthracis* from Stevens' spinal fluid and blood. He is treated with several antibiotics in an attempt to control the infection.

October 5: Robert Stevens becomes the first person to die of inhalational anthrax in the United States in 25 years.

October 7: Anthrax spores are found on Stevens' computer keyboard and in the nose of Ernesto Blanco, the 73-year-old mailroom supervisor at AMI. AMI offices are closed.

October 12: A biopsy of Erin O'Connor's skin rash tests positive for anthrax. New York City Mayor Rudolph Giuliani is notified that there is a case of anthrax in the city. The FBI and city police learn that a second letter postmarked September 18 in Trenton, New Jersey, was received by NBC. The second letter contained a brown granular substance. It is sent to a lab to be tested for anthrax.

October 13: AMI announces that five more people may have been exposed to anthrax. In New York, another NBC employee reports cutaneous anthrax symptoms. Anthrax spores are found in the Trenton letter to NBC.

October 14: A New York City police detective and two Health Department workers involved in the investigation of the NBC letter test positive for anthrax.

October 15: The son of an NBC worker tests positive for cutaneous anthrax. He had been in the NBC office with his mother around the time the anthrax-containing letters had been received. A letter postmarked October 9 in Trenton, New Jersey, and addressed to Senate Majority Leader Tom Daschle tests positive for anthrax (Figure 5.2). Spores are found in the Boca Raton post office.

October 17: Anthrax spores are found on computer keyboards in the offices of New York Governor George Pataki. Tests of his staff are negative for anthrax, but all begin taking the antibiotic ciprofloxacin (brand name Cipro®) as a precaution.

A 55-year-old distribution clerk from the Brentwood postal facility in Washington, D.C., goes to the doctor complaining of muscle aches, weakness, and fever that had lasted about

Figure 5.1 In the wake of the terrorist attacks of September 11, 2002, anthrax-containing letters were mailed to some high ranking officials and news commentators in the United States. Some of those letters passed through the mailroom of a Boca Raton, Florida, office building where several people contracted the disease. In the photo above, FBI agents test the contaminated area.

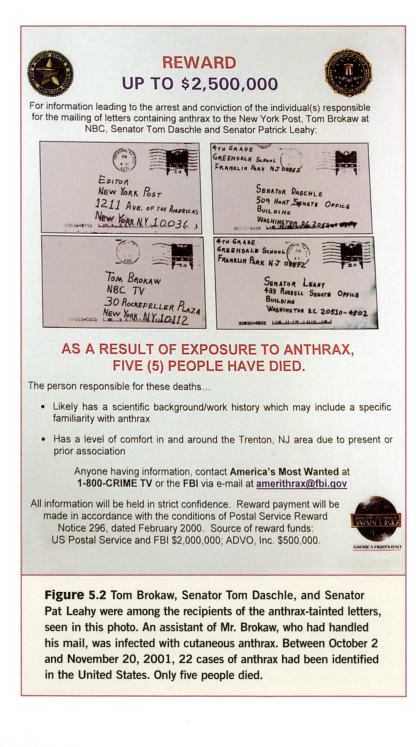

Figure 5.2 Tom Brokaw, Senator Tom Daschle, and Senator Pat Leahy were among the recipients of the anthrax-tainted letters, seen in this photo. An assistant of Mr. Brokaw, who had handled his mail, was infected with cutaneous anthrax. Between October 2 and November 20, 2001, 22 cases of anthrax had been identified in the United States. Only five people died.

a day. The doctor diagnoses a virus and sends him home for bed rest.

October 18: A second 55-year-old postal worker in the Brentwood facility goes to his doctor with a slight fever but normal heart rate and blood pressure. He complains of fever, sweating, muscle aches, and a cough lasting about three days. His doctor diagnoses a viral infection and sends him home.

An assistant to CBS news anchor Dan Rather is diagnosed with cutaneous anthrax. She first noticed a swelling on her face on October 1 and had been unsuccessfully treated with penicillin. Rather's office tests positive for anthrax spores.

October 19: A third postal worker in the Brentwood postal facility goes to the local hospital. He had experienced a sore throat, low-grade fever, chills, headache, and fatigue for about three days. He became short of breath, vomited, and sweated heavily at night.

At the hospital, the postal worker had no fever and his blood pressure and heart rate were normal. His lungs were congested, and a chest X-ray showed a widened mediastinum and fluid in his lungs. *Bacillus anthracis* was isolated from his blood within 11 hours, and he was given antibiotics. His chest cavity had to be drained of fluid several times. He remained in the hospital for several months.

October 20: A fourth Brentwood postal worker goes to the hospital. He has had a headache for about four days, with a fever, chills, sore throat, cough, nausea, muscle aches, sweats, and occasional blurred vision.

At the hospital, he has no fever and his blood pressure is normal. His chest X-ray shows a widened mediastinum and fluid in his lungs, and he is admitted to the hospital. *Bacillus anthracis* is cultured from a sample of his blood within 15 hours, and he is treated with antibiotics. His chest cavity is drained of fluid twice. He is discharged from the hospital on November 9.

October 21: The second postal worker goes to the ER with chest tightness, nausea and vomiting, chills, muscle aches, and shortness of breath. His fever is no higher than before, but his heart rate has increased and he is having trouble breathing. His chest X-ray shows fluid in his lungs that resembles pneumonia, and his heart rate is irregular. He is treated with antibiotics and medication for his heart, but he dies later that day. After he dies, *Bacillus anthracis* is found in his blood.

The first postal worker continues to feel sick, and at 6:00 A.M. on October 21, he goes to the ER (a different one from where the second postal worker went). He is short of breath, weak, and feels pressure behind his breastbone. He also complains of nausea and vomiting, fever and chills, and a cough. His temperature and blood pressure are normal, and he does not appear terribly ill. His heart is beating irregularly, he is dehydrated, and his chest X-ray shows enlarged mediastinal lymph nodes.

Because the hospital staff had heard of two other postal workers suspected of having inhalational anthrax, the man is admitted to the hospital and immediately given antibiotics. In spite of treatment, he dies 13 hours after entering the hospital. *Bacillus anthracis* is isolated from his blood the next day.

October 22: The wife of a Brentwood mail sorter finds him collapsed in the bathroom and calls paramedics. He had complained of "stomach flu" a few days earlier and had fainted in church, but he recovered and went home to bed. He went to work that evening, but after a few hours, his nausea and stomach cramps became worse. He was vomiting and sweating heavily. He had gone to an ER for treatment the day before.

The mail sorter had a lower-than-normal body temperature and low blood pressure. His other signs were normal, and his chest X-ray showed only a slight, possible cloudiness in one small area. The ER physician said he probably had gastroenteritis ("stomach flu") and sent him home, telling him to see his doctor later that day.

When the mail sorter was admitted to the hospital on October 22, he was having trouble breathing, and his temperature and blood pressure were lower than they had been in the ER. Because of two media reports that postal workers had been hospitalized in the Washington, D.C., area with inhalational anthrax, the mail sorter was also diagnosed with anthrax. His chest X-ray now showed a widened mediastinum and fluid leaking into the lungs. *Bacillus anthracis* was found in his blood. Although he was put on large doses of antibiotics immediately, the mail sorter died five hours after he was admitted to the hospital.

October 20: Anthrax spores are found at 13 locations in the Trenton, New Jersey, postal facility. Three workers there test positive for exposure to anthrax.

October 23: Washington authorities announce that two postal workers have died of inhalational anthrax. Health officials advise employees at all 36 Washington postal facilities to be treated for anthrax. The CDC announces that a Trenton postal worker may have inhalational anthrax.

October 24: The postmaster general urges the public to be cautious about opening mail. Three new cases of inhalational anthrax, all linked to the Daschle letter, are reported.

October 25: Homeland Security Chief Tom Ridge announces that the anthrax sent to Senator Daschle was especially pure and highly concentrated. Only a few countries are believed capable of producing such refined anthrax; one of those is the United States.

October 28: A female postal worker at the Hamilton Township Postal Facility near Trenton, New Jersey, tests positive for inhalational anthrax after reporting respiratory symptoms. Anthrax spores are found at the mail facility handling mail for the Justice Department.

October 29: Anthrax is discovered at the Supreme Court, State Department, Health and Human Services building, and an Agriculture Department office in Washington, D.C.

October 31: A New York City woman who worked at a Manhattan hospital dies from inhalational anthrax. A co-worker of the woman and another New Jersey postal worker have cases of suspected cutaneous anthrax. Traces of anthrax are found in postal offices in Indiana and Missouri and in mailbags at the United States Embassy in Lithuania.

November 1: The number of federal buildings where anthrax has been found has increased to 20.

November 16: Officials announce that they have found another anthrax-containing letter similar to the Daschle letter. The second letter is addressed to Senator Patrick Leahy.

November 21: A 94-year-old woman dies of inhalational anthrax at a hospital in Derby, Connecticut. Her blood tests positive for *Bacillus anthracis*. Tests of her home and the other places she had visited recently were negative for anthrax. Some of her junk mail went through the Trenton post office where letters were sent to Senators Tom Daschle and Patrick Leahy. It is presumed that she was exposed while ripping up junk mail that had been contaminated by contact with those letters.

INVESTIGATION

Between October 2 and November 20, 2001, investigators from the CDC and local, state, and federal public health and law enforcement agencies confirmed 22 cases of bioterrorism-related anthrax. Eleven cases were inhalational anthrax (all confirmed); five of these were fatal. Eleven cases were cutaneous anthrax (seven confirmed and four suspected); none of these were fatal.

Four envelopes were recovered containing *Bacillus anthracis* powder. Two envelopes addressed to Tom Brokaw and the editor of the *New York Post* were mailed in or near Trenton, New Jersey, on September 18, 2001. Both envelopes contained letters with the words "9-11-01 . . . "This is next" . . . and "Take your penacillin [misspelling in the letter] now . . . " The letters were processed at the United States Postal Service Trenton postal facility and were sent on to the Morgan Central facility in New York City for sorting and distribution. *Bacillus anthracis* was isolated from both these mail facilities.

The first group of nine cases began about nine days after the first two letters were mailed in Trenton. Seven were cases of cutaneous anthrax in New York City and New Jersey. Of these, five were media company employees or visitors in New York City. Two cases in New Jersey were in postal employees. One New Jersey mail carrier was not exposed to any contaminated work site. He probably was exposed to mail contaminated at another facility.

Two cases of inhalational anthrax in AMI employees in Florida have been included in this group because of the timing of their illness. A co-worker of Robert Stevens recalls him handling a letter containing a fine, white powder on September 19, about a week before he became ill. No contaminated envelopes were recovered in Florida, although *Bacillus anthracis* was found on Stevens' computer keyboard and at several other locations in AMI. *Bacillus anthracis* was also found in several mail facilities through which mail would have been delivered to AMI. All of the people in this first cluster became ill before *Bacillus anthracis* was isolated from Robert Stevens in Florida on October 3.

Envelopes containing anthrax powder were mailed to

SIX LETTERS PROBABLY SPREAD SPORES TO 5,000 MORE

Two researchers developed a mathematical model to study the transmission of *Bacillus anthracis* in September and October of 2001. Their results were published in the *Proceedings of the National Academy of Sciences* in May 2002. They began by assuming that six letters were mailed containing more than ten billion spores each. They also assumed that each letter went through five postal handling facilities where spores could spread to other mail.

Their model suggests that the original six letters (only four have been recovered) could have contaminated as many as 5,100 more on their travels through the postal system. Cross-contaminated letters would have many fewer spores than the original letters, probably between ten and 100 when they reached their destinations. Another 432 letters could have been contaminated with 100–1,000 spores, and 36 letters may have picked up 1,000–10,000 spores.

Two deaths from inhalational anthrax in October and November 2001 have been thought to be due to exposure to cross-contaminated mail because no *Bacillus anthracis* could be found in the patients' homes or, in one case, in the workplace.

The model can be used to predict the consequences of larger-scale attacks, where millions of letters might be contaminated. It also suggests that postal workers might be at high risk for anthrax exposure if spores are mailed.

Senators Tom Daschle and Patrick Leahy in Washington, D.C. The envelopes were postmarked in Trenton, New Jersey, on October 9, 2001. Letters in the envelopes contained the statements "09-11-01 . . . You can not stop us. We have this anthrax. You die now. Are you afraid?"

The second cluster of cases began about five days after the October 9 envelopes were mailed. Five cases of inhalational anthrax in the Washington, D.C., area were in the second cluster. All were in postal workers who were exposed in contaminated mail facilities. Two cutaneous anthrax cases in New York occurred in people who handled the September 18 *New York Post* envelope. Four cases in New Jersey, two inhalational and two cutaneous, occurred in people exposed to anthrax at work. Three of these were postal workers; the fourth was a bookkeeper in a nearby office building. A hospital worker in New York City who died of inhalational anthrax was probably exposed to cross-contaminated mail, as was the 94-year-old Connecticut woman who died in November of inhalational anthrax.

The powder in the October 9 envelopes was finer than in those mailed September 18, resulting in more severe disease. Postal workers were more likely to have been infected from the October 9 letters, even though they did not open the envelopes.

AFTERMATH

The Hart Senate Office Building, located in Washington, D.C., and several postal facilities were closed for decontamination. The buildings were sealed and then chlorine dioxide gas was pumped through the ventilation systems to kill anthrax spores. The entire cleanup cost the federal government $35 million. Millions of pieces of mail never made it to their destinations, including college applications and entrance examination scores.

More than 30,000 people began prophylactic (preventative) antibiotic treatment after the attacks (Figure 5.3). Sixty days of treatment were recommended for 10,300 people. The CDC reported that 44 percent of those interviewed actually completed the 60-day treatment. Of people taking at least one dose of antibiotic, 57 percent reported side effects, mostly gastrointestinal.

Six months after inhaling anthrax spores, several postal workers who survived were still suffering from their experience. *The Washington Post* reported in April 2002 that of the five survivors they interviewed, only the 74-year-old mailroom supervisor at AMI had returned to work. Four others said that even the smallest exertion left them exhausted. They also had problems with concentration and memory.

WHAT WE LEARNED FROM THE 2001 ANTHRAX ATTACKS

The incubation period for inhalational anthrax during the 2001 attacks was 4.5 days, in agreement with previous observations. Early symptoms of inhalational anthrax were those that had been previously described, but in many cases they were difficult to recognize.

The case fatality rate from inhalational anthrax was 45 percent, much lower than would have been predicted. Some people with symptoms could be saved with aggressive antibiotic treatment and supportive therapy.

Sealed envelopes were more dangerous than would have been predicted. Many of those infected with inhalational anthrax were postal workers. However, the overall risk was low. More than 85 million pieces of mail were processed after the October 9 letters with no additional anthrax cases found. Estimates are that someone working near a mail-sorting machine would have been exposed to 30 spores in an eight hour shift.

Figure 5.3 Due to the postal mail related anthrax cases, workers from 36 post offices in Washington, D.C., were tested for the disease. More than 30,000 people were given preventative treatment, even if they did not test positive for the anthrax bacillus. In the photo above, postal workers travel to the hospital for testing.

In March 2002, the family of one dead postal worker filed a $50 million lawsuit against the HMO where he was treated. The HMO had told the worker that he had the flu and sent him home. He died three days later from inhalational anthrax.

Anthrax DNA was recovered from four envelopes, 17 patient samples, and 106 samples from contaminated surfaces. It showed that the anthrax from all sources was identical, probably the Ames strain that had been "weaponized" to reduce the size of the spores and make it easier to spread in the air (see box below).

WHAT'S IN A NAME?

The *Bacillus anthracis* recovered in 2001 from letters, infected people, and buildings was identified as the "Ames" strain. The Ames strain is highly virulent, resistant to many vaccines, and used by military researchers and bioterrorists. For a while, the investigation concentrated on Iowa State University in Ames, Iowa, where an extensive collection of anthrax was located. In response to the investigation, Iowa State University destroyed its anthrax collection. Then it was discovered that the Ames strain was actually isolated in Texas during a cattle anthrax outbreak in 1981.

The mistaken identity occurred when a biologist working at USAMRIID wrote to Texas A&M University researchers asking if they had any anthrax he could use to test the vaccine he was developing. In response to the request, the scientist at Texas A&M mailed a sample of *Bacillus anthracis* from the Texas cattle outbreak to Fort Detrick. Texas A&M often sent samples to the National Veterinary Services Laboratory in Ames using prelabeled boxes. The Texas anthrax sample was mailed to Fort Detrick in one of these boxes, with an additional label directing it to USAMRIID. When the researcher at USAMRIID received the sample he labeled it "Ames," believing it to have come from Iowa.

The "Ames" strain was isolated again in Texas in 1997. It came from a dead goat hundreds of miles away from the 1981 cattle outbreak. Terrorists may need no more than some Texas soil to acquire deadly *Bacillus anthracis* spores.

The FBI and the United States Postal Service offered a $2.5 million reward for information leading to the person who mailed the anthrax-containing letters. Hundreds of interviews with people who had access to anthrax spores or the expertise needed to produce them, as well as at least one search warrant, failed to identify the microbiological terrorist in the year after the attacks.

6

Diagnosing and Treating Anthrax

SIGNS AND SYMPTOMS

Certain signs and symptoms accompany every disease and help the physician with the diagnosis. The *signs* of a disease are the physical changes that the physician can see, like a skin sore or an abnormal chest X-ray. *Symptoms* are changes reported by the patient, such as pain or difficulty breathing.

The signs and symptoms of anthrax resemble those of other diseases. The skin sores in cutaneous anthrax could be infection with *Staphylococcus aureus* or *Pseudomonas* <sude-oh-MOAN-us>, both common human pathogens. They also resemble the bite of the brown recluse spider and cold sores caused by Herpes Simplex Virus. The initial fatigue, fever, and nonproductive cough of inhalational anthrax can resemble influenza or almost any upper respiratory infection. Lung congestion could be pneumonia caused by several bacteria or viruses. The widened mediastinum seen on a chest X-ray in inhalational anthrax could also be caused by occupational exposure to silicon or iron dust. In addition, a widened mediastinum and leakage of fluid and cells into the lung may be difficult to see on initial examination. Many bacteria and viruses also cause vomiting and diarrhea.

In addition, physicians are often taught to follow the adage "When you hear hoof beats, look for horses, not zebras." In other words, they look for commonly occurring diseases, not those that are rare where they practice medicine. With animal vaccination and careful cleaning of imported animal hides, anthrax became a "zebra" disease in the United

States. The terrorist attacks of October 2001 moved anthrax closer to the "horse" category. Physicians around the world exchange information about disease outbreaks to help each other recognize unusual pathogens.

DIRECT OBSERVATION OF *BACILLUS ANTHRACIS*

In the 2001 outbreak, swabbing the noses of people at risk of anthrax exposure sometimes revealed spores, which could be observed under a microscope using a special staining technique.

PROMED-MAIL

In *The Eleventh Plague,* Dr. John Marr, a New York physician and epidemiologist for the New York Department of Health, and his co-author John Baldwin relate a fictional account of a bioterrorist re-creating the Biblical plagues. As the story begins, anthrax kills a boy in San Diego, California. The protagonist of the story is Jack Bryne, moderator of ProMED-mail. Although the story and Jack Bryne are fictional, ProMED-mail functions much as described in the book.

Scientists and physicians created ProMED-mail in 1994 to be a totally public global electronic network for collecting information about disease outbreaks. Moderators screen dozens of reports that come in daily from physicians and public health professionals around the world, organize the reports, and send them out via an E-mail listserv (ProMED-mail) to subscribers. ProMED-mail allows scientists and physicians to benefit from each other's experience in diagnosing and controlling disease outbreaks. It also helps public health professionals recognize outbreaks more quickly by sharing information.

ProMED-mail is a program of the International Society for Infectious Diseases. You can find current postings and links to past messages on the web at *http://www.promedmail.org/.* Anyone may subscribe, although non-professionals must realize that this is not a forum for getting term paper questions answered.

The presence of spores showed that someone had been exposed to anthrax but did not show whether *Bacillus anthracis* had reached their lungs to cause an infection.

At certain times during an anthrax infection, *Bacillus anthracis* may be found in samples of blood or tissue. The sample is placed on a microscope slide and stained with special dyes to show the large rectangular anthrax cells. *Bacillus anthracis* is present in high numbers in blood a few hours before and after death, when many macrophages are dead and *Bacillus anthracis* circulates throughout the body. Early in the infection, *Bacillus anthracis* is confined to the lymph nodes. There may not be enough bacteria present in blood for the cells to be seen directly. Antibiotic treatment also makes it difficult to find *Bacillus anthracis* in blood or tissue samples.

Diagnosis of a bacterial disease is often confirmed by **bacterial culture**: growth of pure colonies in the laboratory. Bacteria are grown in flat plastic dishes called **Petri plates** (Figure 6.1). Inside the Petri plate is a substance with the consistency of gelatin. The **growth medium**, as it is called, contains all the nutrients the bacteria need to grow and divide: sugars for energy, proteins, vitamins and minerals, and salt. It also contains **agar**, a material from marine algae that makes the growth media solid. Agar is also used to thicken jelly and ice cream. The medium may also contain sheep red blood cells to provide extra nutrients. Before it is used to grow bacteria it is sterilized (heated to kill any bacteria that may already have been present). **Sterile** medium will not show bacterial growth unless bacteria are specifically added, for example from patient blood or tissues.

A small amount of patient blood, pleural (lung) fluid, or fluid from a skin sore is picked up with a sterile wire loop and rubbed across the sterile medium. Bacteria in the sample stick to the medium. Each is invisible to the naked eye, but each can grow overnight into a colony of millions of bacterial cells. *Bacillus anthracis* colonies are large (up to

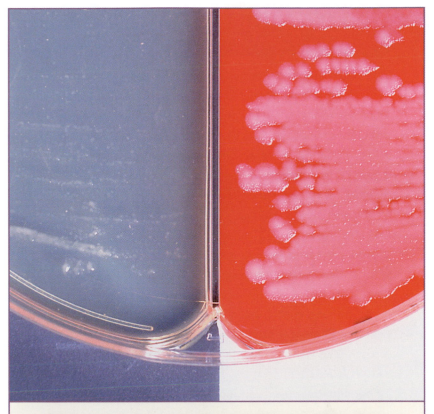

Figure 6.1 Sometimes the anthrax bacteria are present in such a small amount that they can not be detected by viewing the sample under the microscope. To determine whether the bacteria are indeed present, scientists must amplify the number of bacteria in the sample. They do this by growing the culture on a nutritious substance in a Petri dish. In the photo above, *Bacillus anthracis* was grown on two different types of growth media: bicarbonate agar (left) and blood agar (right). Larger colonies formed on the blood agar, which is similar to *Bacillus anthracis*'s preferred environment.

one-eighth of an inch in diameter) and gray-white in color; they may also have irregular edges (Figure 6.1).

Bacillus anthracis is not difficult to grow in the lab but isolating it from patient samples is not always possible. Early in an infection, the numbers of anthrax bacteria in tissue or blood

OTHER BACILLUS SPECIES ("*BACILLUS CEREUS* GROUP")

Three other species of Bacillus can be found in the environment. They also resemble *Bacillus anthracis* when cultured in the laboratory. Because these species are so similar, they are sometimes called the "*Bacillus cereus* group" of organisms. When a Bacillus is isolated from a patient sample, it is important to differentiate *Bacillus anthracis* from the other members of the *Bacillus cereus* group.

Bacillus cereus <serious> can live in the environment and also infect warm-blooded animals, including humans. It produces toxins in food that cause vomiting or diarrhea within a few hours after being eaten, commonly called "food poisoning". *Bacillus cereus* can be found in many types of foods: meats, milk, vegetables, fish, and rice. The best way to prevent food poisoning from *Bacillus cereus* is to cook food well and then keep it very hot or very cold until it is eaten.

Bacillus thuringiensis <thur-in-gee-EN-sis> is an insect pathogen that does not infect humans. When insect larvae eat *Bacillus thuringiensis spores*, toxin crystals in the spores become active Bt-toxin in the insect gut and kill the larvae. Bt-toxin is harmless to humans and animals and only kills certain species of insects. *Bacillus thuringiensis* spores can be sprayed directly on plants to kill larvae. In recent years, scientists have inserted the gene for Bt-toxin into plants, making the plants naturally resistant to insect pests. This allows plants such as corn and cotton to be grown without the use of high levels of pesticides.

The third member of the *Bacillus cereus* group is *Bacillus mycoides* <my-KOID-ees>. *Bacillus mycoides* lives in the environment and is not pathogenic.

may be too low to be recovered. After antibiotic treatment, the bacteria have died and cannot grow in culture. In addition, *Bacillus subtilis* is a common soil bacterium that could get into laboratory cultures from dust. *Bacillus subtilis* looks very similar to *Bacillus anthracis* in culture, so unless anthrax was being considered, the appearance of Bacillus colonies might not seem important and therefore be overlooked.

MOLECULAR TECHNIQUES

Polymerase Chain Reaction (**PCR**) is a more sensitive technique than culture for detecting and identifying *Bacillus anthracis*. PCR can also help scientists to distinguish between *Bacillus anthracis* and other members of the *Bacillus cereus* group. The process involves using small pieces of *Bacillus anthracis* DNA, called **primers**. The primers are added to blood or pleural (lung) fluids that might contain anthrax DNA. Cycles of heating and cooling the DNA allow the primers to **hybridize** (match up) with identical pathogen DNA so that enzymes called **DNA polymerases** can make copies. DNA that does not match the primers will not be copied, so only *Bacillus anthracis* DNA will be made. Once enough copying cycles have occurred, the DNA can be detected by hybridizing it with radioactive *Bacillus anthracis* DNA (Figure 6.2).

In response to *Bacillus anthracis* infection, the body's immune system makes proteins called **antibodies**. Antibodies stick to *Bacillus anthracis*, making the bacteria an easy target for the macrophages to engulf. Antibodies produced to another pathogen will not stick to *Bacillus anthracis*, and antibodies made to *Bacillus anthracis* will not stick to other bacteria. In other words, antibodies are molecule specific. Antibodies to *Bacillus anthracis* can be found in the blood as early as ten days following infection. They are present in the **serum**, the liquid part of the blood that remains after the blood has formed a clot.

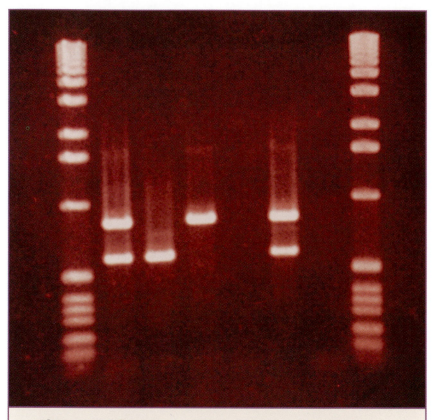

Figure 6.2 Polymerase Chain Reaction (PCR) is one technique that scientists use to isolate specific fragments of DNA. PCR involves using specialized segments of DNA to replicate only the desired sequence in the test DNA. If the specific sequence is not present in the test DNA, no replication will occur. PCR products are then visualized on an agarose gel, like the one pictured above. Each fragment of DNA will be represented by a bar, and the size can be determined by comparing the fragment to a marker of a known size (markers are located in both the first and last lanes of this gel).

The most commonly used test for antibody presence is the **ELISA** (enzyme-linked immunosorbent assay). *Bacillus anthracis* and a sample of patient serum are combined in a special dish. If anthrax-specific antibodies are present in the patient serum, they will stick to the bacteria on the surface of the dish while other serum proteins and antibodies made in other infections will be washed away. Antibodies that are specific for (bind to) the patient antibodies are then added. These **secondary antibodies** are chemically linked to enzymes. Finally, colorless substrate molecules are added and are changed into colored products by the enzymes. The presence of color shows that the patient has antibody to anthrax. With inhalational anthrax, the ELISA test is most useful for confirming an anthrax diagnosis after the patient has recovered or died since antibodies cannot be found early in the infection.

ANTIBIOTIC THERAPY

Antibiotics are chemicals made by microorganisms that kill or block the growth of other microorganisms. Microbes use antibiotics to compete for space and food. Penicillin is an antibiotic produced by a mold, *Penicillium notatum*. *Penicillium* is a common, blue-green mold that you may have seen growing on bread. The British microbiologist Sir Alexander Fleming (Figure 6.3) discovered penicillin in 1929 when he noticed that a colony of mold growing on one of his bacterial cultures had a ring around it in which none of his bacteria could grow. Howard Florey and Ernst Chain at Oxford University later purified penicillin, for which they received the Nobel Prize in Medicine with Fleming in 1945. Penicillin was first commercially produced in the United States during World War II and saved many soldiers from dying of infection.

Most of the antibiotics we currently use come from the mold family *Streptomyces*. They produce the antibiotics streptomycin, erythromycin, neomycin, tetracycline, and gentamycin. The molds *Penicillium* and *Cephalosporium* produce antibiotics (penicillin, griseofulvin, and cephalothin), as do two species of *Bacillus* (bacitracin and polymixin)

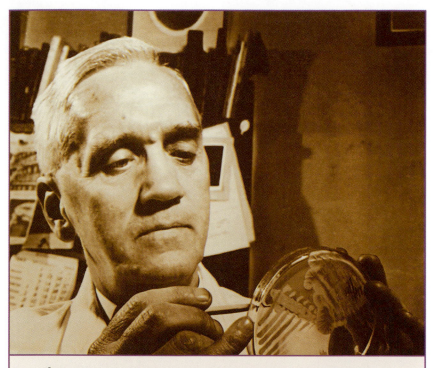

Figure 6.3 Antibiotics are used today to cure a wide range of bacterial infections. Penicillin, the first known antibiotic, was discovered by Sir Alexander Fleming, pictured above, in 1929. Fleming was growing bacterial cultures on Petri dishes when he noticed that one dish contained mold. He also observed that no bacteria were growing near the spot of mold.

Antimicrobials are chemicals synthesized in the laboratory to kill or block the growth of microbes. Many are adaptations of naturally occurring antibiotics, while others are completely new drugs.

Antibiotics and antimicrobials act on microbes in several ways. Some block cell wall synthesis. Since this process occurs in bacteria but not in humans or animals, these antibiotics usually have few side effects. Some antibiotics block the production of other nutrients essential to bacteria but not mammals. Other antibiotics block protein synthesis. Since the cell machinery for making proteins is different in bacteria and in mammals, these antibiotics also have few side effects. Antibiotics that interfere with the structure of the cell membrane have been effective against molds, whose cell membrane has different lipids than mammalian membranes. Antibiotics that block DNA synthesis often interfere with mammalian cell enzymes and have the highest incidence of side effects.

Because viruses use host cell enzymes to produce new viruses, only antimicrobials that interfere with host cell enzyme functions are effective against virus infections, and these have serious side effects. Antibiotics such as penicillin that are designed to interfere with bacterial enzymes are useless against viral infections. In most cases of virus infection, we depend on our immune system to kill the viruses.

Most natural isolates of *Bacillus anthracis* are sensitive to penicillin, an antibiotic with low toxicity and low cost. Penicillin blocks cell wall synthesis. A combination of penicillin and streptomycin (which blocks protein synthesis), works better against *Bacillus anthracis* than either does alone.

Bacillus anthracis is also sensitive to many **broad-spectrum** antibiotics, antibiotics that kill many different kinds of bacteria. Because of the possibility that anthrax used in the bioterrorist attacks of 2001 had been genetically engineered to be resistant to penicillin, ill and exposed people were treated with ciprofloxacin. "Cipro" (as it is commonly known) is a drug in the quinolone family that blocks DNA synthesis. Side effects associated with taking Cipro include nausea, vomiting, diarrhea or stomach pain, headaches, dizziness, fainting, and seizures.

Persons diagnosed with cutaneous anthrax are usually treated for three to five days with oral or injected penicillin. Bacteria in the skin lesions are usually all dead within 24 hours of the start of treatment. Persons diagnosed with inhalational or gastrointestinal anthrax are usually given injected or intravenous antibiotics for six to eight weeks. They may also receive

WHEN ANTIBIOTICS DO NOT WORK

Antibiotic resistance is defined as the inability of an antimicrobial drug to kill or inhibit the growth of a microbe against which it was previously effective. Antibiotics have been very effective against infectious disease when taken as prescribed. However, microbes can become resistant to antibiotics in several ways. Some microbes make enzymes that inactivate the drug. Others make a pump that removes the drug from the cell as fast as it enters. Still others change the enzyme targeted by the drug, so the drug no longer blocks the function of that enzyme.

Microbes resistant to antibiotics appear during infection as mutations (mistakes) occur during DNA replication in dividing microbes. High doses of antibiotics for sufficient time kill all the pathogens, sensitive and resistant alike. Taking too little drug for too short a time allows the resistant pathogens to survive. Resistant pathogens are passed to other individuals. Pathogens can also share antibiotic resistance genes by passing small pieces of DNA called **plasmids** from one pathogen to another. Soon, pathogens that were sensitive to an inexpensive antibiotic like penicillin become resistant and must be treated with a more expensive alternative. Infections with organisms that are likely to become drug resistant (such as HIV) are often treated simultaneously with several antimicrobial drugs (a drug cocktail). Therapy with drug cocktails will not cause antibiotic resistance unless several mutations take place simultaneously, which is much less likely than the occurrence of a single mutation.

A strain of *Staphylococcus aureus* has been found that is resistant to all but one antibiotic. Higher and higher doses of even that antibiotic are becoming necessary to kill the bacterium. Strains of the tuberculosis bacterium *Mycobacterium tuberculosis* that are resistant to all antibiotics are currently infecting people around the world. These people will die because there is no effective therapy for their disease.

vaccinations. People who have symptoms of inhalational anthrax are also treated for shock and difficult breathing.

Prophylactic (preventative) treatment of persons exposed to anthrax with antibiotics proved to be very successful in the 2001 attacks. In general, antibiotics were prescribed for 60 days. The longest known period between exposure to *Bacillus anthracis* and disease symptoms in humans is 43 days. In one primate study, fatal anthrax occurred as long as 98 days after exposure. If exposed and given antibiotics, monkeys became ill if the antibiotics were stopped at 30 days (in one case, 58 days).

People are urged to continue antibiotic therapy for the entire 60 days. Since some of the antibiotics used to treat anthrax have unpleasant side effects, more than half of the people taking prophylactic antibiotics during the 2001 attacks did not complete the full 60 days of treatment. In addition, long term antibiotic therapy can kill normal intestinal flora and allow pathogens to infect these areas, sometimes causing serious gastrointestinal illness.

ANTITOXINS

Neutralizing antibodies against protective antigen (PA) block toxin action by blocking its attachment to the host cell. Neutralizing antibodies against PA from someone who is immune to anthrax have been shown to protect against disease when given to an exposed but unprotected animal or person. This treatment has been used in China, but not in Europe or the United States.

FUTURE THERAPIES

Current antibiotics are very effective against anthrax if given early enough. That could change if terrorists genetically engineer *Bacillus anthracis* to resist antibiotics. Nevertheless, development of new therapies is primarily targeted toward blocking toxin destruction of host cells since toxin can persist even after the bacteria have died. None of these new therapies are ready to be used in humans, but several show promise for the future.

One possible therapy involves the receptor to which toxin must bind in order to enter host cells. This receptor has been identified, and a toxin-binding soluble form of the receptor has been made. As the soluble receptor binds anthrax toxin, it prevents toxin from binding to and entering host cells. Another possible therapy involves making a mutant PA molecule that cannot bind lethal factor or edema factor. The mutant PA competes with the normal PA made by infecting *Bacillus anthracis*, again blocking entry of toxins into the host cell. Animal tests indicate that a single mutant PA molecule might stick to six normal PA molecules and prevent them from making the pore in the host cell membrane

USING VIRUSES TO STOP ANTHRAX

Many bacteria that infect humans have their own pathogens: **bacteriophage**, literally "bacteria eaters." "Phage" <fage> are viruses that infect bacteria. They instruct the infected bacteria to make millions of new phage, then use an enzyme called **lysin** to break open the bacteria and escape to infect other bacteria. As you read this, phage are probably infecting and killing bacteria in your intestines.

Back in the 1930s, Soviet scientists proposed using phage to kill human pathogens. Each kind of phage infects only one kind of bacteria, so phage could be targeted to kill only the pathogen and leave normal flora alone. However, bacteria become resistant to phage as they do to antibiotics, so the idea was abandoned.

Now Dr. Vincent Fischetti and his co-workers at Rockefeller University in New York have isolated lysin from *Bacillus anthracis* and shown that it can be used to kill the bacteria. Purified lysin dropped on bacteria in a test tube kills and breaks them open within 15 minutes. The scientists reported their findings in the August 22, 2002, issue of the scientific journal *Nature*.

Isolated lysin, like the phage, is specific for *Bacillus anthracis*. The scientists tested the enzyme on many bacteria, through which lethal factor and edema factor enter.

An old idea that has shown new promise is the use of bacteriophage, viruses that infect bacteria. "Phage" <fage> use an enzyme called lysin to rupture the bacteria and escape to infect other bacteria. In August 2002, scientists at Rockefeller University in New York announced that they had used lysin from anthrax-infecting phage to kill *Bacillus anthracis* in a test tube. They hope that lysin can eventually be used to kill *Bacillus anthracis* in infected people. When used with another chemical that tricks anthrax spores into becoming vegetative cells, lysin might also work to decontaminate equipment and buildings that harbor anthrax spores.

including *Bacillus thuringiensis*. None of them were harmed. Says Fischetti, "This is beneficial because, unlike antibiotics, this kind of therapy would not kill off useful bacteria in our bodies and thus would have few or no side effects."[5] He also predicts that bacteria would require much longer to become resistant to the lysin than to antibiotics.

Lysin was also tested on mice infected with *Bacillus cereus*, a close relative of *Bacillus anthracis*. *Bacillus cereus* usually kills mice within four hours. When the phage enzyme was injected into the mice 15 minutes after the *Bacillus cereus*, 70 to 80 percent of the mice survived.

The phage enzyme might also be used to decontaminate buildings or to detect and kill anthrax spores, even in people's noses. L-alanine is a germinating agent that tricks *Bacillus anthracis* spores into becoming vegetative cells. Once the spores have become vegetative, they would be killed very quickly by the lysin. The two chemicals could be sprayed together on contaminated surfaces.

5. "Natural-born killers enlisted to fight anthrax," The Rockefeller University Office of Communications and Public Affairs, August 21, 2002. More information at *http://www.rockefeller.edu/pubinfo/082102.php*

7

Anthrax Vaccine

HOW THE IMMUNE SYSTEM FIGHTS BACTERIA

The purpose of the immune system is to protect us from infectious disease.
Cells of the immune system circulate in the blood (white blood cells) and
form collections of tissue called **lymph nodes** and the **spleen**. The spleen
lies in the upper left area of the abdomen near the stomach. It filters
pathogens from the blood and also destroys old red blood cells. Lymph
nodes are found throughout the body, in the lungs and along the digestive
tract, everywhere a pathogen might gain entry. When you have a sore
throat and your "glands" are swollen, these are actually lymph nodes that
are producing more cells to fight the pathogen.

Pathogen molecules are called **antigens**. Antigens can be proteins,
sugars, or lipids. Antigens are part of the pathogen cell or are toxins secreted
by it. Antigens signal the immune system that a pathogen is present by
binding to membrane proteins called receptors on white blood cells.

Macrophages and neutrophils are phagocytes, white blood cells that
engulf and kill pathogens. Their receptors bind antigens that are shared by
many pathogens, so each phagocyte can bind and engulf many different
pathogens. **B cells** and **T cells** are white blood cells that have specialized
receptors. Each B cell or T cell binds only one pathogen antigen, so many
different B and T cells are made to protect us from all the pathogens that
exist. White blood cells communicate using cytokines, small proteins that
are made by one cell and signal another to take some specific action.

We have already seen in Chapter 4 that macrophages are the first line
of defense against *Bacillus anthracis*. When bacteria enter the skin or
lungs, macrophages engulf and destroy them. Macrophages that have
bound bacteria secrete cytokines, proteins that attract neutrophils and

other macrophages to the infection site and make the nearby blood vessels leaky. This allows phagocytes to enter the tissues and eliminate the bacteria. Other macrophage cytokines signal the brain to increase body temperature. **Fever** is a natural defense against bacteria, which grow more slowly at higher temperatures while the white blood cells work better. Complement proteins from the blood coat the bacteria, making them easier for the macrophages to bind and engulf.

If bacteria escape destruction by the phagocytes, they spread to the nearby lymph nodes. Lymph nodes contain macrophages, B cells, and T cells. B cells are produced in the bone marrow, where each developing cell rearranges its DNA so it can make a unique antibody protein. B cells put some of this antibody protein on their membranes as a receptor for antigens. Some B cells will have receptors that bind the bacterium, while others will have receptors that bind toxin.

During an anthrax infection, B cells with receptors that bind *Bacillus anthracis* divide to form a **clone** of identical B cells that make more antibodies, a process that takes several days. They release these antibodies into the blood. Antibodies travel in the blood to the infection site, where they coat the bacteria. Antibody-coated bacteria are easier for the macrophages to engulf and kill, especially if, like *Bacillus anthracis*, they have a sugary capsule. Other B cells make antibodies that bind the anthrax toxins and block them from attaching to and killing cells (neutralizing antibodies). Antibodies remain in the blood for months after the *Bacillus anthracis* is killed. **Memory B cells** that can make antibodies more quickly and in greater amounts if the same pathogen infects a second time are also produced to protect from future infections.

T cells usually help eliminate bacteria like *Bacillus anthracis* that can survive in macrophage vesicles. T cells are produced in the thymus, an organ near the heart. Like B cells, T cells each recognize a different pathogen antigen. Unlike B cells, T cells only recognize small antigen pieces

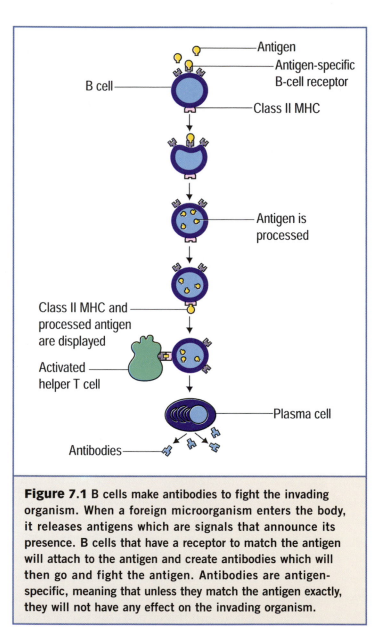

Figure 7.1 B cells make antibodies to fight the invading organism. When a foreign microorganism enters the body, it releases antigens which are signals that announce its presence. B cells that have a receptor to match the antigen will attach to the antigen and create antibodies which will then go and fight the antigen. Antibodies are antigen-specific, meaning that unless they match the antigen exactly, they will not have any effect on the invading organism.

called peptides that have been attached to MHC (major histocompatibility complex) molecules on the surface of specialized antigen-presenting cells. Macrophages and B cells are antigen-presenting cells (Figure 7.1). MHC molecules are the tissue typing antigens that must be matched to prevent rejection of transplanted organs. MHC molecules combine with *Bacillus anthracis* peptides inside the macrophage and carry the peptides to the outside of the macrophage membrane, allowing the T cells to recognize that the macrophage has phagocytosed some *Bacillus anthracis*.

Once T cells bind *Bacillus anthracis* peptides on MHC, the T cells divide to form clones of **helper T cells**. Helper T cells make cytokines to signal macrophages to be better killers of the bacteria they have engulfed. Other helper T cells make cytokines that signal the B cells to make more and better antibodies. Memory T cells are also produced to protect from future attacks by *Bacillus anthracis*.

In the skin, *Bacillus anthracis* can often be contained at the infection site by phagocytes until antibodies are made to neutralize its toxin. Antibody-coated bacteria are engulfed and killed by macrophages with the help of T cells, and the infected person usually recovers. When *Bacillus anthracis* infects the lungs, it spreads to the lymph nodes so rapidly and kills so many macrophages that it can be deadly before neutralizing antibodies are made. *Bacillus anthracis* avoids being killed by the macrophage and uses toxin to kill the macrophages from the inside where it is protected from neutralizing antibodies.

VACCINATION

Vaccination is exposure to a harmless form of the pathogen or toxin that causes the immune system to make antibodies and memory B and T cells that protect against an infection with the virulent pathogen. Although someone who has been vaccinated can be infected by the pathogen, they do not become ill because their immune system responds so quickly that the pathogen is eliminated before it can damage the body enough to cause disease symptoms.

VACCINATION ELIMINATES SMALLPOX

Smallpox virus infects skin cells, forming pustules on the skin that can leave deep scars. It kills 15 to 20 percent of infected people. The Chinese are generally given credit for discovering that taking material from the pustules of an infected person and placing it into a cut on the skin of another often protected the second person from the disease. This process was called **variolation**. Lady Montague, the wife of the British ambassador to Turkey, observed the process of variolation in 1718 and had her son treated. He was protected from smallpox. She urged her friends in Britain to have the procedure performed, and the Royal Society of London sponsored variolation in condemned prisoners. George Washington had his troops variolated during the American Revolution. Variolation protected against smallpox, although two percent of people who were treated died.

Edward Jenner, a country physician in Britain, had observed that milkmaids rarely suffered from smallpox. Instead they contracted a milder skin infection called cowpox from the udders of infected cattle. Jenner used cowpox to protect humans from smallpox. The two viruses are related and share some antigens, so exposure to cowpox induces the production of antibodies and memory B and T cells that protect against the human smallpox virus. He called the process vaccination, using the Latin word *vacca* for cow.

Although vaccination against smallpox became widespread, the disease still killed more than 300,000 people in the twentieth century. In the 1960s, the World Health Organization set the goal of eliminating smallpox. Since smallpox occurs only in humans and all infected people have visible symptoms, the goal was realistic. Wherever smallpox occurred, teams were dispatched to vaccinate everyone who might be exposed. By 1980, smallpox had been eliminated from every country.

Infectious disease is the number one killer of people in the world, and is second in the United States only to automobile accidents. Vaccines have been very successful in reducing the incidence of human and animal disease in the United States and worldwide. We routinely receive vaccinations protecting us from polio, diphtheria, tetanus, whooping cough (pertussis), measles, mumps, rubella, HiB (bacteria that cause meningitis in infants), and hepatitis B. Flu and pneumococcal vaccinations are offered each year to protect us from influenza and pneumonia.

An ideal anthrax vaccine would protect the vaccinated person against illness from all common strains (genetic variants) of *Bacillus anthracis.* The protection would be long lasting, and the vaccination would not have any side effects. The vaccine would also be inexpensive to produce, stable when stored, and easy to administer.

Some vaccines are made of whole pathogens that have been killed or attenuated (weakened) so they will not cause disease but still induce a protective immune response. Other vaccines are made of pathogen antigens that induce immunity without the danger of using whole pathogens. Vaccines currently used in the United States are listed in the box on page 90.

CURRENT ANTHRAX VACCINE

Animal vaccines to *Bacillus anthracis* are made using a strain of the bacterium isolated in 1937. The vaccine strain cannot make a capsule, which reduces its ability to cause disease. It does produce toxins. The vaccine consists of live *Bacillus anthracis* spores that are injected to induce neutralizing antibodies. Live spore vaccines have also been given to humans in China and the former Soviet Union (USSR).

The human anthrax vaccine produced in the United States is made from a strain of *Bacillus anthracis* isolated from cattle. The vaccine strain does not make a capsule or lethal factor, so that it cannot cause disease. Vaccine bacteria are grown in culture, after which the culture is filtered to remove whole bacteria. The cell-free filtrate contains a mixture of *Bacillus anthracis* antigens, including protective antigen (PA). The filtrate is absorbed on to the **adjuvant** aluminum hydroxide (alum). Adjuvant makes the PA easier for B cells to bind and for antigen-presenting cells to show to T cells. All of the United States human vaccine, called anthrax vaccine adsorbed (AVA), has been made by BioPort Corporation at a single facility in Michigan.

HUMAN VACCINES CURRENTLY USED IN THE UNITED STATES

Killed whole pathogens: The intact pathogen is killed and injected. These vaccines are very safe and stable and can result in the production of good neutralizing antibody. They do not induce long-lasting protective immunity against some viruses. Examples: influenza and Salk polio vaccines.

Attenuated whole pathogens: The virus is grown in non-human cells so that it grows less well in human cells and can be injected into humans without causing disease. These vaccines induce better immunity to viruses than do killed vaccines. They can cause serious illness or death in people whose immune systems are weakened by disease or cancer chemotherapy and occasionally may mutate to cause disease in healthy people. Examples: measles, mumps and rubella (MMR), varicella (chicken pox), and Sabin (oral) polio vaccines.

Subunit vaccines: Antigens from the pathogen are injected. These vaccines are very safe because no pathogen is injected. However, they require more boosters and may induce less immunity or shorter-lasting immunity than whole cell vaccines. Subunit vaccines must be accompanied by adjuvant. Examples: DPT (diphtheria, pertussis and tetanus), HiB (*Haemophilus influenzae* B), hepatitis B, and pneumococcal vaccines.

For more information, see the CDC web site at *http://www.cdc.gov.*

To protect against anthrax, the vaccine must be injected under the skin every two months for a total of three injections. Three additional injections are given at six, 12, and 18 months. Annual boosters are given to maintain immunity.

The ability of the vaccine to protect against anthrax was studied in 1962 in mill workers. Participants in the study were divided into three groups: 379 workers received the vaccine, 414 received a **placebo**, and 340 received neither. A placebo is an inactive substance given in the same way as the vaccine. In a successful test, the vaccine should provide protection while the placebo should not. During the study, an anthrax outbreak occurred. Five cases of inhalational anthrax occurred in workers receiving the placebo or no treatment. No cases of anthrax were seen in vaccinated people. In this test and others, the vaccine provided 92.5 percent protection against cutaneous and inhalational anthrax.

The safety of the vaccine has also been studied. Between January 1, 1990, and August 31, 2000, almost two million doses of anthrax vaccine were given in the United States. During that time there were 1,544 reports of side effects (Figure 7.2). Of these, 76 (five percent) were serious, resulting in hospital-ization, permanent disability, or life-threatening illness. Two deaths were reported in vaccinated people, neither due to the vaccine. Other serious side effects, each occurring in fewer than ten people, included pneumonia, seizures, enlargement of the heart, and autoimmune disease where the immune system attacks the body's own tissues. More common side effects, each reported 200 to 300 times, included pain or swelling at the injection site, headache, joint pain, weakness, or itching.

The anthrax vaccine is currently given to people in at-risk occupations, including the military, health-care workers, and public safety personnel (firefighters and police). The United States Department of Defense has an anthrax vaccine web site at *http://www.anthrax.osd.mil/*.

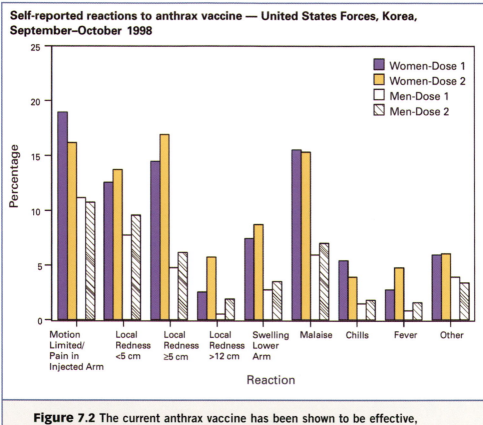

Self-reported reactions to anthrax vaccine — United States Forces, Korea, September–October 1998

Figure 7.2 The current anthrax vaccine has been shown to be effective, with a low percentage of reported side effects. The graph above shows self-reported side effects of the vaccine among United States Forces serving in Korea between September and October of 1998. Limited motion and soreness at the site of the injection were the most common side effects, only experienced by less than 20 percent of the recipients. However, the vaccine involves a relatively long process of injections—three injections over the course of six month and then additional injections at six, 12, and 18 months. Boosters are also required to maintain effectiveness.

FUTURE ANTHRAX VACCINES

Antibodies to PA completely protect against anthrax. They also suppress germination of anthrax spores and help macrophages engulf spores. The role of antibodies against other *Bacillus anthracis* antigens in protecting against anthrax is less clear except in mice, where antibodies against capsules are more important than antibodies against toxins. Other anthrax antigens in the current vaccine may be responsible for the vaccine side effects. Most research on new anthrax vaccines concentrates on producing immunity to PA.

Several new vaccines for anthrax are being tested in animals. Some include a mutated PA that will be unable to bind lethal factor or edema factor, making the vaccine safer but still inducing the production of neutralizing antibodies to PA. Other possible vaccines involve cloning the PA gene into non-pathogenic bacteria or viruses, which would then be injected to induce immunity to PA.

Designing a vaccine to protect against a bioterrorist attack with anthrax might be different than designing a vaccine to protect against exposure to spores on or in animal products. The dose of spores might be higher in an attack, requiring a higher level of protection. A vaccine for use with children might be different than one for use with adults. Since the attacks of 2001, much more attention is being directed to answering these questions.

NEW ANTHRAX VACCINE GETS A GREEN LIGHT

The National Institute of Allergy and Infectious Disease (NIAID) announced on April 18, 2002, that it is seeking bids to develop a new vaccine against anthrax. The federal Department of Health and Human Services will buy 25 million doses to add to nation's emergency stockpile. The new vaccine should require no more than three doses to protect against anthrax. It should also work fast enough so that it could be given after exposure to *Bacillus anthracis*. It will likely include PA. The United States military is also looking for a more effective anthrax vaccine.

8

Anthrax and Bioterrorism

OUTBREAK IN OREGON

It was September 9, 1984, when residents of The Dalles, a town of about 10,000 in the Columbia River Gorge near Mount Hood, began feeling ill. The disease started with mild stomach cramps that became severe. Then chills, fever, vomiting, and diarrhea sent many to the local hospital. So many people became ill that the hospital was forced to put beds in the hallways. The number of ill people declined for a few days and then peaked in a second wave. By the time the outbreak was over, more than 750 people had suffered from the debilitating illness. Fortunately, no one had died.

The Oregon State Public Health Department and the Epidemic Intelligence Service of the CDC questioned hundreds of people and analyzed hundreds of stool samples, trying to trace the source of the illness. The bacterium causing the illness was quickly identified as *Salmonella typhimurium.* Salmonella is a common cause of "food poisoning." The bacterium attaches to the lining of the intestinal tract and makes a toxin that causes nausea and diarrhea.

People became ill after they had eaten in local restaurants. Although the **epidemiologists** could not find a source of contaminated food, they did find that eating food from salad bars was associated with the illness. Restaurant owners willingly closed the salad bars. Food handlers had also become ill, often before restaurant patrons. The public health investigation concluded that the food handlers had not properly washed their hands after using the restroom, then passed their illness along to patrons while preparing salad ingredients.

At the time, residents of The Dalles and surrounding Wasco County were involved in a zoning dispute with the Rajneeshees. The cult, led by Bhagwan Rajneesh, had moved to the area several years before and transformed a remote ranch into a town with a hotel, casino, and disco. Some residents of Wasco Country welcomed the newcomers and the boost to the local economy, while others resented the influx of people with their private police force. By the time the Salmonella outbreak occurred, relations between the Rajneeshees and the townsfolk of The Dalles were unfriendly, and a crucial vote that could decide who controlled county government was coming up. When townsfolk accused the Rajneeshees of somehow poisoning their food, authorities dismissed the idea as paranoia or racism.

A year later, Bhagwan Rajneesh called a press conference to accuse his personal secretary of absconding with money belonging to the sect and deliberately making people ill. The ensuing investigation showed that the secretary, along with the nurse who ran the Rajneeshee medical complex, had purchased Salmonella as part of an elaborate plot to sicken residents of Wasco County and prevent them from voting in the zoning elections.

The biological attack in The Dalles, Oregon, which is described in the book *Germs* by Judith Miller, Stephen Engelberg, and William Broad, occurred 15 years before anthrax in the mail sickened people from Florida to Connecticut. It shows how vulnerable we are to bioterrorism.

LOOKING BACK: A BRIEF HISTORY OF BIOLOGICAL WARFARE

Biological warfare was conducted long before humans knew that microorganisms caused infectious disease. In 1997, several officers from USAMRIID published a historical perspective on biological warfare in the *Journal of the American Medical Association* (JAMA). Documentation of early attempts does not exist, but two outbreaks are often cited as evidence that for centuries humans have used biological weapons against other humans.

In the fourteenth century, the Tartars held the city of Kaffa (in what is now the Ukraine) under siege. When bubonic plague erupted in the Tartar army, they catapulted corpses of plague victims into the city in order to spread the disease to the besieged Kaffans. The plague did infect people in Kaffa, although it is just as likely to have come from flea-infested rats as from the dead.

During the French and Indian War (1754–1763) in the American Colonies, the commander of the British forces, Sir Jeffrey Amherst, suggested using smallpox to kill hostile Native American tribes. When a smallpox epidemic occurred at Fort Pitt (located in what is now Pittsburgh, Pennsylvania) in June of 1763, Captain Ecuyer sent blankets from the hospital to Native Americans. The Indians did get smallpox, although the disease could have been transmitted from contact with the British rather than on the blankets.

During World War I, the Germans infected livestock in several countries exporting animals to the allied troops. They used *Bacillus anthracis* and *Pseudomonas mallei*, the agent that causes glanders (farcy) in horses. More than 200 mules died in 1917–1918. During the same time in suburban Washington, D. C., a German agent who was an American-born graduate of The Johns Hopkins Medical School grew bacteria with which he planned to infect American horses and feed. Humans were not targeted, but human cases increased enough to trigger an investigation by the Public Health Service.

In 1925, the Geneva Protocol for the Prohibition of the Use in War of Asphyxiating, Poisonous or Other Gases, and of Bacteriological Methods of Warfare was negotiated in response to the German use of poison gas in World War I. It prohibited the use of biological agents in war but did not prohibit research or stockpiles of biological weapons. The United States

ANTHRAX ISLAND

In 1942 the British government, fearing biological attacks from Germany, tested its own biological weapons on a remote island off the west coast of Scotland. Winston Churchill was quoted as saying he "didn't see why the devil should have all the best weapons."

Sixty sheep were taken to Gruinard <grin-yard> Island and exposed to a bomb loaded with a "brown, thick gruel" of anthrax spores. The sheep started dying within three days; soon, all were dead.

Gruinard Island seemed a perfect place for the test. Just 520 acres, Gruinard was a mile from the closest house on the mainland yet close to the Allied military base at Loch Ewe. The exact nature of the military exercises was unknown even to the locals for more than 40 years. After a year, the testing stopped, and signs were posted warning people to keep off.

Anthrax did spread to the mainland at least once, apparently when the carcass of a dead sheep washed ashore. At least one horse, one cow, and ten sheep died. The government quickly compensated the owner.

Scientists had assumed that the spores would be washed away or inactivated, but the island remained heavily contaminated for more than 40 years. The experiment proved that anthrax would be a powerful biological weapon.

In 1986 the British government paid Will Kay, a private contractor, £500,000 (about $700,000) to decontaminate the island with formaldehyde and seawater. Said Kay, "I'd never done anything like that before. We were vaccinated against anthrax before we went, but were actually at greater risk from the formaldehyde which is quite difficult to deal with." He found the island rich in wild life and "on a nice day, quite pleasant."[6]

Warning signs were removed, and the island has since been used to graze sheep. Locals go over for picnics or to hunt deer and rabbits.

6. BBC News. "Living with Anthrax Island." November 8, 2001. For more information, see *http://news.bbc.co.uk*

Figure 8.1 During World War II, Great Britain tested anthrax bombs on Gruinard Island. Gruinard Island, (pictured here), is an uninhabited, secluded piece of land off the coast of Scotland. Sixty sheep were placed on the island and exposed to a potent level of anthrax spores. All of the sheep in the experiment died. The experiment was not made public, even though the anthrax spores spread to mainland Scotland at least once. Spores still contaminated the island 40 years later.

did not sign the treaty. Nations that did sign reserved the right to retaliate if biological weapons were used against them.

During World War II, the Japanese tested biological weapons on prisoners of war, including American troops, and used biological weapons on the Chinese. At least 10,000 people died from experiments or execution after experiments were concluded. The scientists who performed the tests were never convicted of war crimes but gave their records to the Americans in return for freedom.

The United States began an offensive biological warfare program in 1942, during which 5,000 bombs filled with *Bacillus anthracis* were produced. Great Britain, an ally of the United States, moved 60 sheep to a deserted island off the west coast of Scotland and dropped an anthrax-filled bomb to test the effectiveness of anthrax as a biological weapon. (See Box: Anthrax Island and Figure 8.1) After World War II was over, Cold War tensions between the United States and the USSR increased. The Cold War was a period of intense political tension between the United States and the USSR, throughout which the threat of war constantly lingered. In the 1950s and 1960s, America and the Soviet Union increased their biological warfare research.

THE COLD WAR: MORE LETHAL BIOLOGICAL WEAPONS

During the Cold War, the center of biowarfare research in the United States was Fort Detrick in Frederick, Maryland. There, researchers worked to improve the transmission and effectiveness of bacteria, viruses, and toxins as agents of war. Scientists at Fort Detrick developed a strain of anthrax so potent that a gallon of culture could kill every man, woman, and child on earth. However, biological agents did not necessarily need to be lethal to be effective weapons. Microbes that incapacitated opposing armies with debilitating diarrhea or headaches would allow troops to win wars without the unfavorable publicity that lethal biological attacks would generate.

Infectious disease agents are attractive weapons for several reasons. They incapacitate or kill people without destroying property. They are invisible and can be spread by air over wide areas of enemy territory. They multiply in their human hosts to infect even people not exposed to the initial attack. Friendly troops can be protected with vaccination or antibiotics, or merely wait until the disease runs its course before entering the area. The primary disadvantage of microbiological weapons is that once they are released from planes or bombs, local wind and weather conditions control their distribution. They are best used on distant targets.

The scientists tested their weapons on conscientious objectors and military troops. They also released "harmless" bacteria into the New York subway system, San Francisco, and other United States cities to test how well the bacteria spread in the air. Because bacterial diseases could be cured with antibiotics, the scientists switched their efforts to using viruses, which are not affected by antibiotics. The scientists perfected growing the viruses in fertilized chicken eggs at the Pine Bluff Arsenal in Arkansas and used them in their tests. By the 1960s, U-2 spy planes showed similar facilities in the Soviet Union. The United States and communist countries accused one another of actually using microbiological weapons, although no use was ever proved.

BIOLOGICAL WARFARE AGENTS

The biological agents weaponized and stockpiled by the United States military until 1973 included bacteria, viruses, and toxins. Of these, lethal agents were *Bacillus anthracis*, botulinum toxin, and *Francisella tularensis*. Botulinum toxin blocks nerve signals to muscles, paralyzing the diaphragm and causing death by asphyxiation. *Francisella tularensis* causes tularemia, with symptoms including fever, muscle aches, joint pain, progressive weakness, and pneumonia. It can be fatal if not treated with antibiotics.

Agents designed to incapacitate were *Brucella suis*, *Coxiella burnetii*, Staphylococcal enterotoxin B, and Venezuelan equine encephalitis virus (VEE). *Brucella suis* causes Brucellosis, a disease with flu-like symptoms. *Coxiella burnetii* causes Q fever, a disease accompanied by a blinding headache, high fever, fatigue, and pain in the muscles, abdomen, and chest. Staphylococcal enterotoxin B causes food poisoning symptoms, primarily vomiting and diarrhea. VEE causes fever and severe headaches and can lead to infection of the central nervous system.

More information about all of these agents can be found on the CDC web site: *http://www.cdc.gov.*

In 1972, the United Nations Convention on the Prohibition of the Development, Production and Stockpiling of Bacteriological (Biological) and Toxin Weapons and on their Destruction (BWC) was negotiated. The BWC prohibits the development, possession, and stockpiling of pathogens or toxins in quantities that could have no protective uses as well as delivery systems for pathogens and toxins. The treaty was ratified by more than 100 nations in 1972 and went into effect in 1975.

President Richard Nixon terminated the United States offensive biological weapons programs in 1969 and 1970. The United States Army Medical Research Institute of Infectious Diseases (USAMRIID) was established to develop diagnostic tests, antibiotics, and vaccines to protect Americans from biological attacks. Although it signed the BWC, the USSR did not immediately halt its biological weapons program, which lead to a deadly accident with anthrax.

AN ACCIDENT AT SVERDLOVSK

Beginning in April 1979 an unusual disease outbreak occurred in Sverdlovsk, USSR (now Yekaterinburg, Russia). Patients arrived at the hospital complaining that their lungs were on fire. Some vomited blood. Most died within 48 hours of becoming ill. Most deaths occurred within two weeks, but some people died nearly six weeks later.

The disease struck men and women ranging from 25 to 68 years old. Interestingly, no children were affected. Altogether, 94 people were infected, and at least 64 people in Sverdlovsk died.

When autopsies were performed on those who had died, their lungs were full of bloody fluid. Many also had bleeding in the brain. Some had hemorrhages in the intestines. Death certificates listed the causes of death as influenza, sepsis (blood poisoning), and pneumonia. *Bacillus anthracis* was recovered from 20 of the 42 who died.

Figure 8.2 Lidia Tretyakova visits the grave of her father, Lazar Karsayev, who was a victim of the Sverdlovsk, USSR, anthrax outbreak. Anthrax spores were accidentally released from a biological weapons plant in 1979 and infected 94 people. The KGB hid the true nature of the disease from the public, stating that the victims had died of other causes. The truth did not surface until the USSR fell apart in the early 1990s.

Soviet authorities blamed the deaths on gastrointestinal anthrax acquired from infected meat. Many animals did die before, during, and after the human anthrax outbreak. The KGB confiscated most of the medical records, but two physicians kept the pathology records and some tissue samples.

When the USSR broke up in 1992, Russian President Boris Yeltsin revealed that the deaths in Sverdlovsk were not due to a natural outbreak. A team of Russian and United States scientists investigated the autopsy records and performed PCR on tissue samples from those who had died. They concluded that an accidental release of anthrax spores from a bioweapons plant in Sverdlovsk was to blame for the anthrax outbreak

(Figure 8.2). The people who died were all downwind from the plant, as were the affected livestock. The release of anthrax spores may have occurred when technicians at the plant briefly forgot to replace an exhaust filter.

Since the breakup of the Soviet Union, it is unclear who has access to weaponized anthrax and where biowarfare research is still going on. The story of Sverdlovsk is told in *Anthrax: The Investigation of a Deadly Outbreak* by Jeanne Guillemin, *Plague Wars* by Tom Mangold and Jeff Goldberg, and *Biohazard*, by Ken Alibek, deputy director of the Soviet biological weapons program.

LOOKING AHEAD: PROTECTING OURSELVES FROM ANTHRAX BIOTERRORISM

Anthrax is a deadly disease, especially the inhalational form. Spores are easy to obtain from soils and the bacteria are easy to grow. Spores are stable, making them easy to store and transport. Only small doses are needed to cause disease. Disease onset is rapid, and inhalational anthrax kills many of its victims. Most people have no immunity to anthrax. Antibiotic-resistant strains could be developed.

However, an anthrax attack would not necessarily be a death sentence for millions of people if public health departments and health-care workers were prepared. It is not spread from person-to-person, so treating and vaccinating exposed people would control outbreaks. Making enough anthrax spores to infect a whole city would require a large facility. Most naturally occurring strains of anthrax are sensitive to antibiotics, and an effective vaccine does exist.

Surveillance is the first line of defense against microbiological weapons. Health-care workers must be trained to think of diseases that might be intentionally spread when they examine patients with infections. Quicker diagnostic tests, as well as equipment to detect anthrax in the environment, will allow for rapid treatment and containment of an outbreak. In March 2002, *The Washington Post* reported that two manufacturing firms are working on devices that will vacuum up spores in high speed mail sorters and detect them using PCR technology. The equipment will also detect seven other biohazards.

Prevention is another defense against deadly anthrax. Following the 2001 outbreak, the United States Postal Service bought eight "e-beam" irradiation machines. The machines use high voltage electron beams to kill bacteria. Half were to be installed in the Washington, D.C., area and half elsewhere to kill spores on mail.

A device originally invented for growing plants in space may be adapted to kill anthrax spores. The Wisconsin Center for Space Automation and Robotics developed a device to remove ethylene from the air. Leaves of growing plants release

A PIECE OF HISTORY

In the late 1970s, many of the research buildings at Fort Detrick had been converted from biowarfare research into cancer research labs. Some were still sealed, full of deadly anthrax spores from the biological warfare work that had gone on there in the 1940s, 1950s, and 1960s. Across the base, USAMRIID investigated deadly microbes, not as offensive weapons but to learn how Americans might be protected from possible attacks. Down the road, the satellite dish that was the hot line to Moscow pointed at the heavens. Surrounding the base, fields of sentinel cattle still kept watch. They would be the first to get anthrax if it escaped.

One day a rumor flew through the cancer center that the air handling unit from one of the anthrax labs was going to be removed and buried. Curious scientists gathered in the parking lot to watch a helicopter hover over a distant building, cables dangling. Finally the bulky unit was lifted and carried off to an undisclosed location. A piece of history had been put to rest.

ethylene. It hastens ripening and decay of fruits. The device uses a titanium dioxide film and UV light to convert the ethylene to CO_2 and H_2O. Spores can also attach to the film and be killed by UV irradiation. Tests with *Bacillus subtilis* show that for every 1,000 spores sucked into the device, fewer than 100 emerged.

Promising experiments on new treatments for anthrax and a more effective vaccine are underway. New methods for anthrax treatment and prevention offer hope for the future. However, better human intelligence and awareness of groups that might be prepared to use anthrax as weapons may offer our best defense against another attack.

Glossary

Adjuvant—Substance given with a vaccine antigen to make it more potent.

Agar—A solidifying agent for bacterial growth media. Also used to thicken some food products such as ice cream.

Antibiotic—Molecule made by one microbe that kills or inhibits the growth of another microbe.

Antibiotic Resistance—Acquired insensitivity to an antibiotic to which the microbe was previously sensitive.

Antibody (pl. **antibodies**)—A protein made by B cells in response to antigen. An antibody specifically binds only the antigen to which it was made.

Antigen—Molecule on a microbe to which the immune system responds.

Antimicrobial—(drug) Laboratory-made drug that kills or blocks the growth of microbes. Often called an antibiotic, although technically antibiotics are made by microbes, and antimicrobials are synthesized in the lab.

Attenuate—Weaken. An attenuated microbe cannot cause disease.

B cells—Immune system cells that make antibodies in response to a microbe antigen.

Bacterial culture—Growth of bacteria in the laboratory.

Bacterium (pl. **bacteria**)—A microbe that can live free in nature or infect plants or animals.

Bacteriophage—A virus that infects a bacterium. Also called a phage.

Broad-spectrum antibiotics—Antibiotics that kill many different kinds of bacteria.

Capsule—Sugary coating around a bacterium that protects it from phagocytosis.

Carrier—Someone who has a disease without having symptoms. A disease carrier can unknowingly infect others.

Clone—An exact copy or many exact copies.

Colony—The descendents of a single bacterium, large enough to see without a microscope.

106

Complement—Group of proteins in the blood that help the body eliminate microbes.

Cutaneous <cue-TANE-ee-us>—Involving the skin.

Cytokine <SITE-oh-kine>—Chemical signal made by white blood cells.

Cytosol <SITE-oh-soll>—The gel-like material inside cells, surrounded by a membrane.

Daughter cells—Offspring of cells. Each bacterial cell divides to form two identical daughter cells.

Disease incidence—Number of cases of disease in a particular span of time.

Disease reservoir—Place where infectious microbes live between disease outbreaks.

DNA hybridization—The technique of allowing single strands of DNA to form double strands with matching DNA.

DNA polymerase—Enzyme that copies DNA.

Edema <eh-DEE-ma>—Swelling caused by fluid leaking from the blood circulation into the tissues.

Edema Factor (EF)—One of the toxins made by *Bacillus anthracis*. When edema factor combines with protective antigen, it is called edema toxin.

Edema Toxin (EdTx)—The toxin formed by the combination of edema factor and protective antigen.

ELISA (enzyme-linked immunosorbent assay)—Test for antibodies.

Enterotoxins—Bacterial toxins that damage the cells of the intestinal lining, causing fluid loss and diarrhea

Epidemiologist—Person who investigates the spread of an infectious disease.

Etiology <ee-tee-OL-oh-gee>—Cause of a disease.

Exotoxin—A bacterial toxin that leaves the bacterial cell and can spread in the blood to other parts of the body.

Fever—A controlled increase in body temperature that helps fight disease.

Fungus (pl. **fungi**)—A mold: one of the life forms that can cause disease in humans. Fungi may be microscopic like yeasts or large like mushrooms.

Germination—The process by which a spore becomes an actively growing, vegetative bacterial cell.

Growth medium (pl. **media**)—The nutrients on which bacterial colonies are grown in the laboratory.

Helper T cells—Immune system cells that make cytokines to enable B cells to make antibodies.

Host—The human, plant, or animal infected by a pathogen.

Hybridize—see **DNA Hybridization**.

Immune system—The body system that fights infectious disease.

Incidence—Number of cases of a disease.

Intoxication—In microbiology, the poisoning of host cells by bacterial toxins.

Intravenous <intra-VEEN-us>—Given directly into a vein.

Lethal Factor (**LF**)—One of the toxins made by *Bacillus anthracis*. When lethal factor combines with protective antigen, it is called lethal toxin.

Lethal Toxin (**LeTx**)—The toxin formed by the combination of lethal factor and protective antigen.

Lymph nodes—Collection of immune system cells that filters microbes from the tissues and contains white blood cells that recognize and fight the pathogen.

Lysin—Phage enzyme that breaks open host bacteria to release newly made phage.

Macrophage <macro-FAGE>—White blood cell that engulfs and kills microbes.

Mediastinum <media-STINE-um> (adj. **mediastinal**)—middle of the chest, the location of the mediastinal lymph nodes infected in inhalational anthrax.

Memory cells—B cells and T cells that have been previously exposed to an antigen and can now respond faster and more effectively in response to another encounter.

Meningitis <men-in-JITE-us>—Infection of the membranes covering the brain and spinal cord.

Microbe <MIKE-robe>—An organism too small to be seen without a microscope; a microorganism.

Microbiology—The study of microbes—viruses, bacteria, fungi, and protozoan parasites.

Micron—Unit for measuring microbes. One micron (micrometer) is a millionth of a meter.

Neurotoxin—Toxin that damages tissues of the nervous system

Neutralizing antibodies—Antibodies that block binding of toxins to host cells.

Nonproductive cough—No material from the lungs is coughed up.

Normal flora—Microbes that normally live on and in the body without causing disease.

Obligate pathogen—A microbe that must live in a human or animal host.

Opportunistic pathogens—Microbes that normally live outside the body or as normal flora and only cause disease when they enter the body accidentally.

Pathogen <PATH-oh-jen>—Microbe that causes disease.

Petri plate—Plastic lidded dish in which bacteria are grown in the laboratory.

Phage <FAGE>—A bacterial virus (bacteriophage).

Phagocytes <FAG-oh-sites>—White blood cells that engulf and kill microbes.

Placebo <pla-CEE-bo>—A treatment that resembles the actual treatment but has no active ingredient. Placebos are used as comparisons for testing vaccines and medications.

Plasmids—Small pieces of DNA separate from bacterial DNA that can be transferred between bacterial cells.

Polymerase Chain Reaction (**PCR**)—Procedure that allows a researcher to specifically copy pathogen DNA, so that very small numbers of pathogens can be detected.

Primers—Small pieces of pathogen DNA used for PCR.

Prophylactic—Preventative. Prophylactic antibiotics are given before disease symptoms are present to prevent the disease from occurring.

Protective antigen (PA)—Protein made by Bacillus anthracis that makes a pore in the host cell, allowing lethal factor and edema factor to enter and kill the cell.

Protozoan parasites—Similar to amebas, one of the life forms that can cause disease in humans.

Pseudopodia <sude-oh-PODE-ee-ah>—The finger-like projections used by phagocytes to surround and engulf microbes.

Pure culture—Growth of bacteria in the laboratory in the absence of other microbes.

Ragpicker's disease—An old name for inhalation anthrax.

Receptors—Cell surface molecules that bind antigen or toxin.

Secondary antibodies—Used in the ELISA test for patient antibodies to anthrax. Secondary antibodies specifically bind human antibody molecules and are linked with enzyme molecules.

Serum—The liquid remaining after blood has clotted.

Spleen—Collection of immune system cells that filters microbes from the blood and contains white blood cells that recognize and fight the pathogen.

Spontaneous generation—The theory that living things could arise from non-living things, like maggots spontaneously appearing on meat or microbes spontaneously growing in fermenting fruit juice.

Spore—A thick-walled resting form of a bacterium that can survive in the environment for many decades. Under the right conditions, spores "hatch" to become vegetative cells.

Sterile—Without any living microbes.

Superoxides—Oxygen compounds that phagocytes use to kill microbes.

T cells—Immune system cells that help macrophages kill bacteria they have engulfed and help B cells make antibody.

Vaccine (adj. **Vaccination**)—Harmless form of a pathogen or antigen that induces a protective response by the immune system.

Variolation—A historic method of protecting against smallpox by scratching live smallpox virus into the skin.

Vegetative cell—A growing and dividing bacterial cell; not a spore.

Vesicle—A bubble inside a cell. A phagocytic vesicle contains microbes that have been engulfed by a phagocyte.

Virulent <VEER-you-lent>—Causing disease.

Virus <VY-rus>—A very small microbe that must live inside animal or plant cells, often causes disease.

Woolsorter's disease—An old name for inhalational anthrax.

Zoonosis <zoo-oh-NO-sis> (pl. **zoonoses** adj. **zoonotic** <zoo-oh-NOT-ik>)—A disease that can be transmitted from animals to humans.

Further Reading

Alibeck, K. 1999. *Biohazard.* New York: Dell Publishing Co.

Bartlett, J. J. "Applying Lessons Learned from Anthrax Case History to Other Scenarios." *Emerging Infectious Diseases* 5:561, 1999. Available at *http://www.cdc.gov*

Beck, Raymond W. *A Chronology of Microbiology in Historical Context.* Washington, D.C.: ASM Press. 2000.

Brock, T. D. *Milestones in Microbiology: 1546 to 1940.* Washington, D.C.: ASM Press. 1999.

Clancy, T. *Rainbow Six.* New York: Berkley Books. 1999.

Clark, W. R. *At War Within: The Double-Edged Sword of Immunity.* New York: Oxford University Press. 1995.

De Kruif, P. *The Microbe Hunters.* New York: Harcourt, Brace and Co. 1926.

Dixon, T. C., M. Meselson, G. Guillemin, and P. C. Hanna. "Anthrax." *The New England Journal of Medicine.* (1999) 341:815.

Emerging Infectious Diseases. (October 2002) The entire issue of the journal is devoted to discussing bioterrorism-related anthrax. Available at *http://www.cdc.gov.*

"Epidemiologic Notes and Reports of Human Cutaneous Anthrax – North Carolina, 1987." *MMWR* Vol. 37, (July 8, 1988) p. 413. Available at *http://www.cdc.gov.*

Garrett, L. *The Coming Plague: Newly Emerging Diseases in a World Out of Balance.* New York: Penguin USA. 1995.

Guillemin, J. *Anthrax: The Investigation of a Deadly Outbreak.* Berkeley, CA.: University of California Press. 1999.

"Human Anthrax Associated With an Epizootic Among Livestock – North Dakota, 2000." *MMWR.* Vol. 50 (August 17, 2001) p. 677. Available at *http://www.cdc.gov.*

"Human Ingestion of Bacillus Anthracis-Contaminated Meat – Minnesota, August 2000." *MMWR.* Vol. 49 (September 15, 2000) p. 813. Available at *http://www.cdc.gov.*

Inglesby, Thomas V. "Anthrax: A Possible Case History." *Emerging Infectious Diseases* 5: 1999. 556. Available at *http://www.cdc.gov*

Marr, J. S. and J. Baldwin. *The Eleventh Plague.* New York: HarperCollins Publishers. 1998.

Mangold, T. and J. Goldberg. *Plague Wars: A True Story of Biological Warfare.* New York: St. Martin's Press. 1999.

Miller, J., E. Engelberg and W. Broad. *Germs: Biological Weapons and America's Secret War.* New York: Simon and Schuster. 1999.

Oldstone, M. B. A. *Viruses, Plagues and History.* New York: Oxford University Press. 1998.

Osterholm, M. and J. Schwartz. *Living Terrors: What America Needs to Know to Survive the Coming Bioterrorist Catastrophe.* New York: Delacorte Press. 2000.

Preston, R. *The Cobra Event.* New York: Random House. 1997.

Regis, E. *The Biology of Doom: The History of America's Secret Germ Warfare Project.* New York: Henry Holt and Co. 1999.

Turnbull, P. C. B. *Guidelines for the Surveillance and Control of Anthrax in Human and Animals.* 3rd edition. World Health Organization. 1998. Available at *http://www.who.int/en*

Young, J. A. T., and R. J. Collier. "Attacking Anthrax." *Scientific American* (March, 2002).

Websites

Anthrax Facts. American Veterinary Medical Association.
http://www.avma.org

Anthrax Vaccine Information Program. Web Site of the
    Department of Defense.
http://www.anthrax.osd.mil/

Biological Warfare Agents (Partial List). Federation
    of American Scientists.
http://www.fas.org/nuke/intro/bw/agent.htm

Bioterrorism. U.S. Food And Drug Administration.
www.fda.gov/oc/opacom/hottopics/bioterrorism.html

Centers for Disease Control and Prevention.
http://www.cdc.gov

Cohn, David V. (1996) The Life and Times of
    Louis Pasteur.
http://www.louisville.edu/library/ekstrom/special/
    pasteur/cohn.html

Genetically Modified Corn Exudes Toxin. Natural Science.
http://naturalscience.com/ns/cover/cover11.htm

Health Aspects of Biological and Chemical Weapons.
    World Health Organization.
http://www.who.int/emc/deliberate_epi.html

History of Biowarfare.
http://www.pbs.org/wgbh/nova/bioterror/history.html

Microbial Spore Formation. American Society
    for Microbiology.
http://www.microbe.org/microbes/spores.asp

Overview of Zoonoses. County of Los Angeles,
  Department of Health Services.
http://phps2.dhs.co.la.ca.us/vet/guides/vetzooman.htm.

Biography of Robert Koch. Nobel e-Museum.
http://www.nobel.se/medicine/laureates/1905/koch-bio.html

Index

of gastrointestinal
anthrax, 37
of inhalational anthrax,
39-40, 49-50, 52,
54-55, 56, 59, 60,
61, 70
and toxins, 51-53, 52
Smallpox, 96
Soil, spores in, 42-45
Sores
in cutaneous anthrax,
19, 35-36, 49, 50, 70
in gastrointestinal
anthrax, 37
Soviet Union, and biological warfare, 99, 100,
101-103
Spleen, 84
Spores, 23
devices killing, 104-105
as disease reservoirs,
42-45
in gastrointestinal
anthrax, 37
and transmission of
animal anthrax,
28-30, 31
Sterile medium, 72
Stevens, Robert, 55-56, 64
Streptomyces, 77
Streptomycin, 79
Superoxides, 47, 49, 52
Surveillance, 103
Susceptibility, to animal
anthrax, 36
Sverdlovsk, USSR, anthrax
accident in, 101-103
Swelling
in cutaneous anthrax,
36
in gastrointestinal
anthrax, 37

Tartars, 96
T cells, 84, 85-86, 87
Thymus, 85
Toxins, 51-53, 87

Transmission
of animal anthrax, 28-
30, 31, 32
from animals to
humans, 32, 36, 45
of cutaneous anthrax,
34, 36
from humans to
humans, 32
from infected meat, 32,
37
Treatment of anthrax, 77-83
and antitoxins, 81
and case study on possi-
bility of attack, 13,
14, 15, 16
and future, 81-83, 105
See also Antibiotics
Trenton, New Jersey Postal
Facility, and 2001
Anthrax Attacks, 54, 56,
61, 62, 65
2001 Anthrax Attacks, 17,
54-69
aftermath of, 65-69, 104
and American Media,
Inc., 54-55, 56, 63-
64, 66
and anthrax vaccine, 93
and antibiotics, 56, 59,
61, 66, 79, 81
in Brentwood Postal
Facility, 56, 59-61
and Tom Brokaw, 54, 63
and CBS, 59
cutaneous anthrax in,
54, 56, 59, 62, 63
and Tom Daschle, 56,
61, 62, 65
deaths in, 55, 60, 61, 62,
63, 67
in Derby, Connecticut,
62, 65
diagnosis of anthrax in,
71
in Hamilton Township
Postal Facility, 62

inhalational anthrax in,
39, 42, 54-55, 56,
59-61, 62, 63, 65,
67
and investigation, 63-
65
and lawsuits, 67
and Patrick Leahy, 62,
65
and NBC, 54, 56, 63
in New York City, 54,
56, 62, 63, 65
and *New York Post*, 63
and outbreak, 54-56,
59-62
prologue to, 54
and Dan Rather, 59
in Trenton, New Jersey
Postal Facility, 54,
56, 61, 62, 65
in Washington, D.C.,
56-61, 62, 65
and weaponized
anthrax, 68

United Nations Convention
on the Prohibition of the
Development, Produc-
tion and Stockpiling
of Bacteriological
(Biological) and Toxin
Weapons and on their
Destruction, 101
United States, and biologi-
cal warfare, 96, 98-101
United States Army
Medical Research
Institute of Infectious
Diseases, 12, 95, 101
United States Postal
Service. *See* 2001
Anthrax Attacks

Vaccination, 87, 89
and Pasteur, 24-25
See also Anthrax vaccine
Vegetative cells, 47

Picture Credits

About the Author

Janet Decker grew up in a small town in Michigan, planning a nursing career. Then, while in high school, she attended a summer microbiology course sponsored by the University of Michigan and the National Science Foundation. A picture of a virus with its DNA coiled next to it changed her career plans.

Dr. Decker received her B.S. in Microbiology from the University of Michigan in 1968 and her Ph.D. from UCLA in 1974. She was a National Multiple Sclerosis Society Postdoctoral Fellow at the Walter and Eliza Hall Institute for Medical Research in Melbourne, Australia from 1974–1977. From 1977–1980, she was a scientist at the Frederick Cancer Research Center at Fort Detrick, Maryland, where she and her husband often picnicked just down the road from USAMRIID and witnessed the removal of the anthrax-contaminated air-handling unit described in this book.

Dr. Decker is the author of scientific papers in the field of immunology and of the review text *Introduction to Immunology*, published by Blackwell Science in 2000. She lives in Tucson, Arizona, with her husband and teenage daughter. There, she teaches immunology and microbiology as a senior lecturer in the Department of Veterinary Science and Microbiology at the University of Arizona.

About the Editor

The late I. Edward Alcamo was a Distinguished Teaching Professor of Microbiology at the State University of New York at Farmingdale. Alcamo studied biology at Iona College in New York and earned his M.S. and Ph.D. degrees in microbiology at St. John's University, also in New York. He taught at Farmingdale for over 30 years. In 2000, Alcamo won the Carski Award for Distinguished Teaching in Microbiology, the highest honor for microbiology teachers in the United States. He was a member of the American Society for Microbiology, the National Association of Biology Teachers, and the American Medical Writers Association. Alcamo authored numerous books on the subjects of microbiology, AIDS, and DNA technology as well as the award-winning textbook *Fundamentals of Microbiology*, now in its sixth edition.